The Nervous Hostess Cookbook

The Comforting Companion to Worry-Free Entertaining

Magic Moments,
Great Friends,

Ursula Bacon

The Nervous Hostess Cookbook

The Comforting Companion to Worry-Free Entertaining

Hostessing Savvy, Memorable Table Settings,
Delicious Prepare-Ahead Menus for All Occasions

Ursula Bacon

BookPartners, Inc.
Wilsonville, Oregon

BookPartners, Inc.
P.O. Box 922
Wilsonville, Oregon 97070

To Thorn, always.

The act of bringing people together is an art and can be compared to painting a picture, weaving a tapestry, or writing a poem.

A piece of art is a medley of colors, textures and form blended to express a thought, an idea or a moment.

A dinner party is much the same.

Ursula Bacon

Acknowledgments

Even though I have come to call the recipes in this book "mine," most of them probably had their beginnings somewhere else. They could well have been born in my mother's kitchen or created in a friend's home. They may have had their origin in someone's favorite cookbook, followed me home from a dinner party or picnic, or appeared on the pages of a food magazine. Over the years of preparing these recipes, they have gone through many changes: they have been added to, reduced here, enhanced there, doubled in size, peppered more, salted less, herbed and garlicked, soaked in wine, and rendered tiddly with brandy. Who knows? I take credit only for what they are today.

Marian Guertin, American chef, restaurateur and most innovative creator of fine foods, assured me that — like anything else — "There's nothing new under the sun." She also remarked that people who experiment with herbs and condiments in the preparation of food are bound to come up with similar results.

Since I have no means by which to trace the origins of these recipes — most of them go back more years than I care to admit to — I wish to express my gratitude to everyone who has contributed to my treasure trove of culinary expressions:

To Escoffier and Chef Hèrcules — *merci beaucoup*. And then there is Frau Holland, Liesel, Katrinka — *danke schön*. To *Julia-Julia, Bon Gourmet, Tante Pasta, Parmesan n' Vino,* and *Better Ovens* magazines. To my mother, all my neighbors — former and present — my friends, my kitchen witches, pot watchers, self-appointed tasters and nibblers — thank you for your contributions.

And a million thanks to all of you who never let up on me — who relentlessly bugged and nagged me, who threatened me with a gloomy future of fallen soufflés and rancid ravioli unless I finished my book.

I've finished!

Thank you so much!

Now, let's have dinner!

Here's to:
"Evenings that begin in delight and end in wisdom."
– Robert Frost

Table of Contents

Introduction

*If time, so fleeting must like humans die, let it
be filled with good food and good talk, and then
embodied in the perfume of conviviality.*
— M.F.K. Fisher, The Art of Eating

From the start, right here at the very beginning, I want to make something very clear: I am not Martha Perfect. Come to think of it, we're not even nodding acquaintances. I don't grow designer carrots all of the same size. I don't have a Neiman's greenhouse — inside or out. (It's one of those economic conditions with which I'm forced to live.) I don't weave my own ribbons from Irish moss, nor do I call green beans *haricots vert*. I have had my share of kitchen disasters, dinner-table tragedies and living-room crises. I have ruined meals, broken dishes, spilled red wine on snowy linens, dropped dinner for six on the carpet, forgot I invited dinner guests, had the wrong date, and lost two false fingernails in the *pot au feu*.

I have cooked pasta so long that it turned to glue. I have burnt garlic bread to a crisp, turned expensive juicy beef roasts into hardball material, and I've forgotten to serve the vegetables — more than once! I have had *gateaux de chocolade* fall so low they bottomed out. I've forgotten to serve my hot dinner rolls, and left them in the oven until they matured into lethal weapons of the third kind. I have literally torched those precious, fragile *Crêpes Suzette* with brandy flames so high the dining room ceiling had to be painted. I dropped a contact lens into the martini pitcher and never found it, and I still can't pronounce *crudités*. I've done all that and more, and prevailed.

The best you can do is to laugh off your mistakes and clean them up. If you only knew what goes on behind the scenes in Martha Perfect's kitchen, you wouldn't feel at all bad about your mini boo-boos. You'd giggle your head off and — just like Martha — put on your Wellingtons and become house designer of outdoor cookware for the Tackytown chain.

Then there is always the unexpected — the things that usually happen at someone else's party. I remember the night when a couple I had known for several years started divorce preliminaries right in the middle of my living room, which did nothing for my so-called well-planned, harmonious evening. I finally convinced them to take their preliminaries home. Later I discovered that the ill-fated couple got divorced at someone else's house at a Sunday brunch, which I believe is more appropriate than at dinner. Of course, some people never do get divorced; they just threaten, and ruin their friends' parties with their bickering and winged insults.

Another time, two (gentle)men got into a fistfight in the study over something that had nothing to do with anything, got blood on the white carpet, tore out of the house, and apparently headed for the nearest ER, never to return — at least not to my house. I suppose I should be grateful for that.

Then there was the occasion my centerpiece caught on fire when a candle exploded and nearly destroyed a guest's Hong Kong-beaded cashmere sweater. Eager and full of Boy Scout vigor, one of the guests tossed a glass of water at my more-than-surprised friend. Talk about a change in the conversation — it was sizzling and smoldering, to say the least.

How can I not remember the day our power was turned off without a warning one hour before our guests were due to arrive, just because I had forgotten to pay the electric bill? I still think I should have won some outstanding-acting award for convincing the power company representative to turn the electricity back on, stop by to pick up the check, and stay for dinner.

Fortunately, that was before computers answered the telephone at utility companies and put you on hold. I got to talk to a live woman who understood what would happen to a soufflé in a cold oven. Her name was Miriam. I have named my famous no-fail chocolate soufflé after her — in French, of course — *Soufflé Chocolade Pour Miriam.* Have you noticed how much more prestigious foods are and how much better they taste when you can't pronounce them?

I just wanted to clear the air and present my dubious credentials for writing a book about entertaining, because I not only do it all the time, but I love it. And I make mistakes. Every time I think I've learned something from a successful evening, I may get a swollen head. Every time I learn something from a disaster, I get downright humble.

All I want to achieve in these pages is to help you take the fear out of entertaining and get to the the bottom of what it's all about:

I want to share my ideas on equal rights for the hostess.

I want to help make cooking easy and successful.

I want to convey in simple terms the sense of joy that comes from experiencing a grand evening.

I want to help you laugh about your mistakes, convince you not to cry over lumpy gravy, give you confidence in your talents, and make hostessing what it should be: FUN. It won't be anything like Martha Perfect, but then the world won't miss another recipe for fennel-glazed prime rib in an apricot-blush puff pastry shirt served with shredded potato *tutu à la Turandot*.

I want the contents of this little book to be a rousing toast to good friends, a celebration of every circle of festive spirits, and a lasting compliment to moments beyond the ordinary.

A votre Santè! Prosit! Chin-Chin! Salut! Le Chaim! Cheers!

Chapter One

About Dinners with Fairies and the End of Magic

It's really better to invite all the dull people one night and all the bright ones the next. The dull won't know it's dull because it's always that way.
– Peg Bracken
The I Hate to Cook Almanack

Years ago, Lady Constanza, seasoned hostess, wife of a true-blue British diplomat in China, offered me the best advice about entertaining guests I have ever had.

In her cozy, chintz-covered, flower-filled living room, over a cup of fragrant tea, she imparted her wisdom in her clipped and precise English voice: "All you have to do is bring the right people together, my dear, create an atmosphere to compliment your guests, and help them shine their own light."

With a conspiratory chuckle she added, "Of course, you must fill your house with flowers and candlelight.

Candlelight is so flattering, you know," she sighed, as if pleased with her discovery.

"Entertaining is NOT about food," Lady Constanza continued to instruct, "so keep the menu simple, spend time with your guests — get out of the kitchen — and stay in control — ever so subtly, of course!"

The dear lady's words sounded like a tall order: complicated, detail-ridden and overly ambitious, and even a tad bit stuffy at the time. What made it a little difficult for me to swallow her expert advice was the fact that she had never even put on as much as a tea party for a flock of flower fairies, not to mention real people, with her own manicured, snowy hands. After all, that was the job for her servants. And she had plenty of them. Actually, Lady Constanza had never seen the inside of a kitchen, although it was rumored that she had a general idea of its location. This fine lady knew which side of her English muffin was buttered.

But what she did with consummate skill was to carefully put together her guest list, plan the menu, supervise the table settings, and see to it that the rest of her house was in order. As they say in the South, "She knew how to do!" It was under her meticulous direction that her party preparations blossomed and burst into full bloom with the arrival of her guests. She saw to the comfort of her friends, made sure the conversation flowed smoothly — and on top of that, she had a smashing good time herself. Needless to say, it doesn't hurt to have help.

It was several years later when the time came for me to entertain in my own home in America, and I was ready — servants or not. I remembered her words and faithfully followed her suggestions for one simple reason: I had seen her in action; I knew her ideas worked.

Later on in my life, Pearl Mesta's tongue-in-cheek comment confirmed my well-rooted suspicions about entertaining, when she quipped, "Don't invite a bore to dinner — just send him one!"

The famous "Hostess with the Mostess," as she was referred to — the subject of the sparkling Broadway play, *Call Me Madam* — a master at creating the most intriguing and exciting parties of the fifties and sixties, knew what she was talking about. Don't invite a bore! Don't be like Dame Edith Sitwell, who complained, "I'm one of these unhappy persons who inspire bores to the greatest flight of art." Well, think about it.

What hostess needs the lampshade-on-his-head calypso dancer stumbling around her living room spilling drinks and breaking things? Who wants a true-confession-bad-luck Suzie falling apart between the salad and the main course? And what contribution to a dinner party is conversation dominated by someone's urge to discuss her aunt's gallbladder operation — aided by another guest's recounting of the latest blood-and-guts episode from a hospital television show?

Thanks for sharing, folks! But that's not my kind of evening, and I don't believe it's yours, either. For purely selfish reasons, I like to have a good time at my own parties. It makes it worth the effort, time and money that go into preparing for an evening of entertaining. I have called myself a compulsive hostess and a recreational cook. Some people like to knit, read the stars or take flying lessons. I love to entertain — it's safer than flying and a more exact science than practicing astrology.

However, I give a lot of thought to planning an evening. I don't invite the Hatfields and the McCoys just to find out who's the best shot. My living room is not a sparring ground for duelling couples, and I refuse to practice marriage counseling without a license. I like congenial, interesting people who enjoy exploring ideas and like good conversation. I like people with a quick sense of humor who get a kick out of a sprinkling of tall tales, who are serious about dreaming, and who love good company, soft music and candlelight. Of course, they appreciate good food — but that's not all of why they come.

I have fun creating table settings that range from whimsical to elegant to downright silly — depending on the occasion. The meals I serve don't require exhausting culinary cartwheels and are not nearly as photogenic as the images on the pages of *Bon Gusto*. I have no intention of running a neck-and-neck race with the chefs of Lutece, Le Grenouille, Table d'Hote, or any other high-flying eatery with a fancy label. I figure if I can't pronounce the name of the restaurant to begin with, I'm bound to be a flop at reading the menu.

I have learned a great deal from people and about people. I discovered that most human beings love a festive mood. They gladly move out of the ordinary settings of daily life into a few moments of special charm. The people I know appreciate provocative and lively conversations more than they care for a five-star meal. Once people are challenged to leave the confines of practiced social small talk, they become fascinated with the adventure of opening the doors that lead to exploring new ideas as they test and stretch their imaginations. There's nothing duller than the empty prattle of Who said what? Did what? Went where? Cost how much? And woe is me!

This book is for the woman who doesn't know where to start. It's for the woman who is not just reluctant, but downright panicky about entertaining for a variety of reasons — of which there are many. At the same time, I am inviting the tortured heroines of mass entertaining — even though they shudder at the thought of having another one of those big once-a-year-you-all-come bashes, and wish they didn't have to — to try a few of those special, small dinner parties that can be ever so much more rewarding. Give it a roll, ladies — you might enjoy it. I bet you a *Crème Brûlée* you will!

I'd rather face a French firing squad shooting candied garlic capers at me than invite all my friends at the same time — not that I have that many. And as far as my enemies go — well, if I have more than four, I take two out to lunch.

Perhaps this book will also help those nervous hostesses who have to face the more complicated prospects of entertaining bosses, clients or business associates. Friction and tension, as well as personal and professional differences, not only ruin an evening but may result in fallout at the office or in the boardroom.

I urge you to be especially careful in the planning of business-related events. Learn as much as you can before-hand about your guests in order to eliminate foreseeable problems, which can range from food allergies or "hate-broccoli" syndromes to, "Oh, no … there he goes again with his dirty stories." More challenging for a hostess to redirect — but high on the list — are conversations that irritate, insult and bring to a quick boil a guest's political, personal or religious convictions. It's too bad people don't leave their biases and inflated opinions at home or, even better, just dump them altogether.

It's up to the host or hostess to take the sting out of conversations and rescue equanimity without ruffling feelings. A quick interference with a joke, a handstand, the spilling of an innocent glass of water (not on the guests, just on the carpet), can provide the pause to steer the conversation skillfully to safer ground.

It has been my experience that it is best to invite no more than four people from "the office" at one time. By limiting the number, you can forestall conversational alliances that may lead to touchy subjects. It is amazing how quickly most people respond to a good laugh, a change of pace, and most are usually willing and swift to dive happily into a new and less volatile topic. If you're prepared, vigilant and aware of your hostess power, the event you have dreaded may just turn out to be a grand evening.

If you have a guest in your living room who stubbornly holds onto a temper-raising point like a dog to his soup bone, you may have to be more direct and face him with a brief "Drop-It" between clenched teeth and flashing red warning lights in your eyes. You may also "drop" a heavy paperweight on his foot, dump a glass of water in his lap, or invite him into the kitchen to take the garbage out, then lock the door behind him — by mistake, of course.

Those moments will become rarer and rarer in your hostessing career as you become more and more selective about bringing people together — for their pleasure and yours.

Every time I look at the animated faces at my dinner table, I believe that the energy, the mirth and the thought-provoking conversation that circle among us like birds on the wing can change someone's world for the better. When the evening is over, when we hang around the hall for lengthy goodbyes, and reluctantly part, I feel great. And when I turn out the lights, blow out the last candle, straighten the pillows on the couch, and glance at the quiet and empty rooms, I can still hear the warmth of laughter, recall snatches of some grandiose idea, and bathe in the glow that good friends leave behind.

"It was a splendid evening, indeed," I muse to myself.

I want you to be able to say that at the end of every one of your parties — you deserve it! I do not make light of the effort that goes into cleaning and cooking and preparing for a dinner party, but all that work is wasted if the guests do not blend well, and the conversation threatens to spoil the evening.

Keep in mind that your guests are the major players when you invite them to dinner. They are the stars. The rest is easy. If you have any doubts about entertaining, if you're like so many women I know who ... "prefer a new edition of the Spanish Inquisition" to entertaining at home, this friendly book takes you by the hand and guides you through the steps for preparing your house, your table and your menus. You don't have to be Martha Perfect (with a staff of eighty), gold-leaf your brownies, and still have time to have your picture taken. There's no need to make your own candles from clarified beeswax, or bonsai your free-range chickens to pass for Cornish game hens in order to be a great hostess. Of course not.

All you have to do is learn a few tricks and adopt some clever shortcuts to organize your life. You'll learn to serve delicious, prepare-ahead, attractively presented meals and discover ways to create a warm and hospitable atmosphere. If you remember to keep it simple, you'll be surprised at how easily you can pull off a dinner party — and have fun.

❧ ❧ ❧

There are twenty-two dinner menus and a few super-casual kitchen dinners in this book, plus a couple of summer picnics, a quick, delicious luncheon, and three winter holiday feasts. Side dishes are interchangeable with most of the main courses. I have made an ironclad rule never to experiment with a new recipe the day of a dinner party. I suggest you try the menus in this book once before you prepare them for your guests — just to get the hang of them.

I have served the meals I'm offering in the recipe section for years, to the delight of my guests. I am often asked to share the recipes. I gladly oblige, but I warn my friends that these time-tested recipes are my standard entertaining menus, and I'll serve them again and again. I never have to worry how a meal turns out — God knows I've prepared them often enough.

I keep a little blue — or red or green or purple — book (the eleventh edition by now) where I enter the date of the dinner party, who came, what I served, and what kind of evening we had. That way I can rotate my menu choices for variety and move my guests around in case I discover a poor fit. Sound a bit too technical? Maybe so — but it works for me, and takes but a moment. (You can do it during TV commercials unless, of course, you are already doing something else during those precious few minutes.)

Don't forget to have fresh flowers for the table and the house! And don't cry over lumpy gravy. (Here's a simple cure for lumps: throw the mess into the blender on high speed for a minute or so, and those offending lumps will be annihilated.) Plan the meals you feel good about preparing, and remember Julia and her nonchalant, what-the-hell kitchen tactics, mindful of where they have gotten her!

Polly, a good friend of mine, used to go into a purple coma at the very thought of entertaining. "I can't cook like you," she'd moan, her face ashen, her hands shredding a worn-out Kleenex into confetti. "The only thing I ever do that's any good is a pot roast," she complained, "and that's not very chic, is it?"

Well, it may not be chic — but who cares for chic as long as it's delicious? Martha Perfect isn't coming to dinner. She was last seen polishing high-desert apple seeds with a cloth of handwoven New England woggle sprouts for her hen-pecked pickle party.

If pot roast is all you feel comfortable preparing, because you know it's terrific, that's okay. You will earn the reputation of being the Pot Roast Queen, and people will fall all over themselves to get to your table. I know I would. My friend took my advice. Now known as "Pot Roast Polly," she never varies her menu and has collected quite a following. What I forgot to mention is that Polly is a sparkling, witty and charming woman. Once she got the fear of cooking out of her system, concentrated on her guests and set the scene for entertaining, she was on her way.

At the risk at repeating myself — just as I do with my menus — I insist that blending the right people, creating a warm ambience of ease and casual festiveness, aided by a good measure of sparkling conversation, makes for a memorable dinner party — food is secondary.

❦ ❦ ❦

I am fortunate to have grown up in a family where entertaining was the breath of life, the number one pleasure. Although I can't duplicate those glorious parties in the stately homes of my various family members, I can harness the spirit, the very essence of entertaining, and transport it into my vastly different and much simpler world.

But, magic is magic, and I create my own.

I was born in Germany just about the time when the country of Goethe, Schiller and Beethoven was taken over by Adolf Hitler and his not-so-merry men. Some people's lives were affected immediately. Others, steadfast in their belief in the basic decency of their countrymen who supported the Nazis, waited for things to change and life to return to sanity. Finally, as reality dawned and their vision cleared, thousands jumped at every opportunity to start new lives in unknown, faraway places. The fate of the rest — all six million of them — was shackled to a master design of destruction beyond their comprehension. They became the dust and ashes of Germany's soul — a mute monument to man's inhumanity to man, and to God himself. Almost at the last minute, and with a lot of help from friends and family, my parents did manage to escape from Germany. I was young when our lifestyle came to an abrupt halt, and things changed drastically.

However, before the madness touched our lives, I had witnessed so many wonderful goings-on that forever would I remember the excitement and character of the festive occasions, which found their perfect settings in villas and venerable old country estates. These were the rambling houses several uncles and aunts of mine called home. By the time I was three years old, I had become the "weekend kid" for three of my father's sisters whose marriages had remained childless. With Albert the chauffeur, resplendent in his dark green livery behind the wheel of one of my uncle's prize Mercedes, or by private railway car (acquired by my eccentric grandfather under questionable circumstances, so my mother insisted), I was hauled all over the countryside and parts of Europe, accompanied by my nanny, Fräulein Charlotte. Eventually, I would be welcomed by one of my perfumed aunts, who greeted me with a peck on the cheek and good words. I guess I qualified as the original "Rent-a-Kid."

I loved every minute of these visits, even though I was left to my own amusement almost moments after I arrived. I was hugged by my weekend-mother after I handed over the hostess gift — usually a large box of rich Belgian chocolates my mother had provided — was asked a few strange questions adults seem to think are appropriate for easy communication with children, and promptly directed to one of the guest suites, accompanied by Fräulein Charlotte. My weekend aunt would give instructions of what time to appear for lunch or dress for dinner, then would be on her way to one of her "important things to do".

I was not in the least upset by being abandoned. I loved to wander from room to room, from floor to floor, and look with wonder at all the treasures I found. There were statues and paintings to be admired, intricate carvings on chairs and chests to be traced with my fingers, and catching my reflection in all kinds of mirrors that were as old as they were big. But the real bonus came when Fräulein Charlotte napped or was involved in one of her big books — she did a lot of that. I'd steal my way into the kitchen where Frau Holland, head cook and pastry genius, in all her ample, robust glory was the unopposed queen of the realm.

She was quite an act. Her strong hands with their blunt fingers were like deep fluttering shadows coaxing, punching, caressing, teasing a hunk of dough until she was satisfied with the "feel" of it. She'd toss and sprinkle dashes of this, that and the other into bowls and pans with seemingly wild abandon. She rarely measured anything.

Whether she was tasting a sauce or the makings of a soup with her wooden spoon, or checking the consistency of a dough, a soufflé mixture, or the stuffing for a duck, her head was always tilted back, her eyes tightly shut and her face calm. She seemed in a trance. Maybe she was the channel for Escoffier and was awaiting "input" from the great kitchen in the sky. I was in awe of Frau Holland, who was considered the pride and joy of Schloss Kleinfeld, my aunt Helene's country home.

Perched on a tall stool, draped in one of Liesel's aprons, I watched the chopping and grating, the searing and stirring, kneading and rolling. One of the big black ovens — large enough to accommodate almost the whole length of a deer and a brace of pheasants at the same time — was reserved for roasting meat, fowl and side dishes. A special oven was used for bread and pastry baking. Heated with a combination of wood and coals, the ovens kept the huge cellars and their thick stone walls warm and cozy all winter long.

Kitchen helpers Katrinka, Liesel, Minna or Marie — I knew all their names — would clear a corner of the massive, scrubbed-white, hundred-year-old kitchen table, and hand me some dough and wooden utensils to keep me busy until Fräulein Nanny discovered my presence in off-limits quarters and sent me scuttling up the stairs, reprimanding me for smelling like a kitchen maid. I found nothing wrong with that. I sure liked the aroma of baking and cooking better than the cloying sweetness of Fräulein's favorite toilet water.

In comparison to the grand style of some of my uncles and aunts, my parents' life was somewhat simpler, less glamorous and grandiose, but there was always time for entertaining friends. Except for a few special occasions in which the big houses were filled with people, dinner parties ranged from six to no more than twelve guests. But regardless of the number, the care and decorum that went into the preparations for an evening of entertaining never varied.

My favorite times as a weekend rent-a-child were spent with Aunt Antonia and Uncle Erich, who lived in a square, spacious, three-story seventeenth-century country estate where celebrations, dinners and formal balls occurred all year long, in tune with the seasons, as regularly as the changing of foliage in the park-like grounds. The colorful hunt ball was followed by several special harvest celebrations. There were winter balls and sleigh rides on starry, crystal-clear winter nights, followed by venison dinners that concluded with the playing of clever parlor games, readings from favorite authors, lively discussions, or the telling of highly amusing stories — all to the soft sounds of music in the background. Christmas Eve dinners were spectacular and steeped in the Christmas tradition of an era that is lost in time and of which only fragments remain.

In summer, Japanese paper lanterns of all shapes and colors, lit by candles, added their glow to late-night garden parties. Tables were set on the broad stone walk that circled the big pond where exuberant frogs competed with the musicians and hip-plopped from one lily pad to the next, doing their own version of table hopping. All year long, small dinners, followed by a friendly game of bridge, were a common practice, as was dressing for dinner.

Summer and winter, there were always a few house-guests ready to enjoy a lavish "country" breakfast — hearty enough to send Kellogg's cornflakes lovers running for bicarbonate of soda and fat-gram-guardians running for the tofu. Caviar and pâté nestled in chilled, glass-lined silver trays and bowls. Slices of delicate, smoked goose breast, Westphalia

ham and fine sausages competed with glistening slices of
pale-pink lox, smoked eel and flounder on colorful beds of
greens. The only healthy offerings on the big platter of
Stilton, brie and double-cream cheeses were thick slices of
apple and clusters of grapes. The rest of the breakfast dishes
were prepared with generous amounts of butter, gallons of
cream, and were sauced to oblivion. Cholesterol was unheard
of, rich food was king, and dieting was for the poor chaps
afflicted by an attack of gout, or those starving pencil-thin
mannequins in the salons of French *haute couture.*

In the afternoon, while Fräulein Nanny napped
soundly, I padded into the dining room that had been
prepared for the evening's festivities. I remember how I'd
slowly circle the beautifully set table on tiptoes, enchanted
with the soft glow of the antique silver pieces, the dull sheen
of the damask tablecloth, as I gawked at the mysterious
array of crystal goblets lined up at precise angles at each
place setting.

There were always surprise treasures amid the flowers
and the heavy silver candelabra with their tall, white tapers.
Sometimes the table was scattered with my aunt's collection
of silver birds and strutting peacocks, which in fall were
replaced by an assembly of hand-painted porcelain
pheasants in brilliant colors and a scattering of fine china
quail. Sometimes the table came alive with amusing,
whimsical pieces of hand-carved ivory and alabaster, or
Auntie's horde of delicate Meissen figurines. Behind each
lovely place setting, fragile, silver filigree easels held a
single flower, like a flag, drawing attention to the gold-
edged parchment place card which beckoned each guest to
his spot at the table.

I never gave a thought to the wonderful food that
would eventually grace the table. Just the way everything

looked and sparkled and winked was fairyland and enough for me.

I would stand behind the hostess's chair and smile at my imaginary guests. With my flannel nightie turned into gossamer silks, I would wave my magic wand — a strip of willow branch — in the air, casting a spell that would hold onto the glittering night, invite my favorite flower fairies to their seats, and conjure up magical moments.

Later at night, again with the reassuring sounds of Fräulein Nanny's burbly snoring coming from her quarters next to my room, I would sneak out of bed once more, tiptoe down part of the huge stairway, snuggle against the thickly carpeted steps, and look down at the grand hall where beautifully gowned ladies and handsome men in black and white attire listened to musical offerings, and sipped coffee from delicate Sèvres demitasses which the venerable Mr. Lothar and his helpers passed around on handsome old Russian silver trays.

I remember the brilliant flashes of light that danced off the huge crystal chandeliers with their countless glittering bulbs and prisms as they mingled with the tiny bursts of colors coming from the lavish display of the ladies' jewels. I listened to poetry readings rendered by deep male voices, the silvery sing-song of baroque music performed by a quartet. Sometimes there were the bell-like sounds of a woman's clear soprano voice singing a favorite melody, or the mood became wistful with the soft plunkings of a harp. It was all so wonderful, and I had the best seat in the house.

There always seemed to be purpose to the festivities, another dimension that went far beyond the combination of people and food. And there was always music, conviviality and joy. There were flickering candles in soft, shadowy corners. Vases and stone urns overflowed with fragrant flowers everywhere. Shimmering streaks of rainbow lights bounced off the sharp ridges of cut crystal. There was magic in the air.

I knew that when I grew up, I would be just like my glamorous aunts or my lovely mother, arranging for and presiding over such glittering nights and festive tables surrounded by animated faces, jeweled gowns and the heavenly sounds of music and laughter.

But man plans, and God laughs. Little girls may dream, but they wake up to a different reality. It was March 1939. My parents fled Germany overnight, finally paying heed to the ugly threats of a mad king. The magic disappeared forever. Life became a matter of survival. The music, the laughter and the warm glow of festivities vanished in the harsh confines of a Japanese detention camp in Shanghai, China, two years after we landed in the last "open port" on the face of the earth.

My parents and I spent the last four years of World War II in a Japanese-controlled "Designated Area" for stateless refugees, along with 18,000 other middle-Europeans, referred to as "Displaced Persons."

Gone were the spacious rooms of the splendid manor houses, the sparkling chandeliers, the paintings of old Dutch masters in their ornate frames glowing richly against the pale hues of the thick walls in high-ceilinged rooms. Nothing was left of the warmth of the ruby-red Turkish carpets with their intricate patterns and sprinkling of brilliant colors. There were no more massive Georgian silver pieces, huge crystal bowls and epergnes to catch their reflection in tall, massive gold-framed Venetian mirrors.

Gone was the collection of romantic antiques, the silken chairs and satiny settees. There were no more people in festive garb to laugh and drink strong, black coffee from tiny golden cups, or sip champagne from delicate crystal flutes. Vanished were the nannies to teach me, to scold and to reprimand, and to inhibit me from living in my self-made magic. Everyone, everything was gone. Gone forever.

Chapter Two

Life Went the Other Way

When you have two loaves of bread,
Sell one and buy a lily.
                    – author unknown

Our little family lived in the nine-by-twelve part of a larger room that had been divided to accommodate two families. The building was a typical, narrow Chinese rowhouse located in the poorest, rat-infested, filth-heaped, disease-riddled part of Shanghai, among thousands of locals. The flimsy wooden partition, promising an uncertain privacy, barely separated our lives from those of the older German couple who made their home in the larger of the two rooms. The makeshift wall stopped three feet short of the ceiling, allowing the activities of two adults and their child to mingle indiscriminately with the uncensored living sounds of those on the opposite side. I had to learn a lot of lessons in thoughtfulness and consideration — whether they were reciprocated or not.

Our small room was furnished with a cheap backless and armless couch, a stiff easy chair that made into a narrow bed, and a thin plywood cupboard to hold our pitiful belongings. Dad slept on the undersized, flimsy couch that barely accommodated his tall frame. Mother made her bed in the dubious comforts of the fold-out chair that soon got lumpy from use. When my parents were settled in for the night, I set up an old cot in the space left between the foot of the couch, the extended chair and the cupboard. Only the deep darkness of the night hushed the regular breathing of my sleeping partners and managed to provide me with a false sense of solitude.

With my eyes shut against the ugliness of our new world, I would call into being my favorite places at home in the gardens, the tea parties with my dolls in the gazebo, sleigh rides in the thick of winter, and always, always, the grandiose parties with all their irresistible brilliance of colors and sounds. I dreamt of the kitchens back home, the smells, the tastes and the comfort of it all.

I dreamt of Lotte and Minna and Katrinka chopping fresh green vegetables, peeling crisp apples and fixing meals. I had visions of Frau Holland kneading and pounding fragrant dough, creating sumptuous cakes, pastries and good breads. I dreamt of home and Aunt Antonia's house. I smelled the simmering of a rich stew, the comforting aroma of yeast rising. I heard the clinking and clattering of dishes amid the laughter and giggles of the kitchen helpers. I dreamt of everything that we had left behind. But the night ended and, with it, the dreams.

Every morning, I woke up to the harsh and guttural cries of a Chinese coolie announcing his immediate arrival to collect the contents of the dozens of small wooden barrel-like pots filled to overflowing with human excrement. They were put out by us and others the night before in the narrow lanes. I lost count of the irritating, annoying mosquito bites that covered my arms and neck in the summer, and the nasty, angry, red bumps an army of hideous bedbugs left behind on the rest of me — all over my body, all year long.

The four small, random pieces of china and crystal that mother had managed to carry in her suitcase from one continent to the other remained in full view on the wooden box that served as our all-purpose table, until we had to trade them in for food during our last months in the detention camp. In all the ugliness, filth and hopelessness of our new home, with a devastating war raging across the globe, disease and death around us daily, these few pieces of crystal and two books of poetry were the icons of our lost yesterday world. They served as reminders of a lovely time, confirming that beauty and grace did indeed exist.

With an admirable combination of strength and Jewish resignation, Mother held together the fragile strings of our hearts. She kept tight reins on our fears and apprehensions, and talked of … "when we return to … when we go back to … when this is over … when … when … all will be well." Little did she know that those magic times and special places would never be a part of our lives again.

She never let up on her display of good manners, and tenaciously held on to traditions — fragmented and incomplete as they may have been. They were the discipline and the reliable customs upon which our lives had been given substance, and she must have known how important a sense of continuity was to us. Ballgowns were carefully taken apart and made into more common garments — underwear for Dad, blouses, slips and nightgowns, curtains and tablecloths. All of these things Mother sewed by hand, while my father was out and about scrounging for "opportunities," which could translate into a piece of homemade salami, a pound of moldy rice or an ounce or two of grey, wet sugar.

Our meals may have consisted of several pounds of cooked potatoes, a vegetable stew with strange transparent noodles, or a hunk of thick, dark bread, but the table was set with a treasured piece of linen, hand-washed almost daily by my mother. With a clumsy black-as-night iron equipped with a thick, wooden handle, its belly filled with glowing hot charcoal, she pressed the linens silky smooth, often leaving her with nasty burns from exploding bits of coals that landed on her arms and hands.

Mother cut two large, snowy-white damask dinner napkins, which had mysteriously escaped with us, into four squares, each of which she patiently hand-hemmed with even, tiny stitches to increase our supply of napery. The woman, who had once presided over dozens of outlandishly large tablecloths woven to her specifications, matching napkins and yards of of priceless Venetian and Belgian lace, was thrilled to own four small pieces of damask.

Bits of tough, weedy greenery that grew in the plaster cracks below our window, or leaves from a bamboo plant that poked a few slim shoots through a fence, were carefully plucked to share a small crystal vase with two pale, slightly faded, pink silk roses rescued from a long-forgotten ballgown.

Mother insisted that "things taste better when the table looks pretty." And we needed a lot of "pretty" to face daily the tired menu of strange and un-gourmet accidents we called food.

Our stove consisted of a clay pot — about the size of a large flower pot — fitted with a grate in its middle to hold charcoal. A small, square opening near the bottom of the pot provided the necessary draft to keep the coals going. I took

turns with Mother, squatting Chinese-fashion on our
haunches, fanning the coals to keep the food cooking.
Careful or not, with clock-like regularity we would pass out
from inhaling the fumes of the burning charcoal. A heavy
dizziness would slowly spread over us from head to toe, and
soon our legs buckled and we'd pass out for several
minutes. Revived by a hefty sniff of ammonia, we'd resume
our cooking chores — soon to pass out again.

"Entertaining" friends was still a life requirement, but
it became less than a minor production. People got together
for a cup of tea and a handful of peanuts — all served on
odd pieces of Sevres or Meissen. (It tasted better!) Our few
friends didn't come for tea and peanuts; they came to talk,
to exchange ideas, philosophize, explore the endless regions
of the universe, to recite poetry or read a passage from a
favorite master. Mother never permitted discussions about
"our condition." She firmly believed that talking wouldn't
make things any better, and speaking about our predicament
would only dig us deeper into the black hole of despair.

The worst she ever said about our exile was, "It's the
land of smiles, gone a bit sour," referring to one of her
favorite operas, Lehar's *The Land of Smiles,* which takes
place in China.

Typhoons raged in the spring, whipping refuse and
people alike all over the city, flooding alleys and streets
with putrid water from backed-up sewers. Oblivious to the
wet conditions underfoot, rickshaw coolies sloshed ankle-
deep in filthy, disease-infested waters, pulling their human
loads from here to there. Winter brought us a bone-chilling
dampness that clung in glistening beads of moisture to our
faces and clothes.

The summer's "tiger" heat, combined with the
strength-sapping humidity, left us gasping for fresh air.

Limp and covered with a fine film of perspiration night and day, our ill-fed bodies became easy targets for tropical diseases. Our intestinal problems were a daily matter of discussion as we compared notes on the cause and effect of the "Asian Quickstep."

Through all the misery, the discomforts, the Japanese occupation, our confinement, and a seemingly endless war, my father's spirit never wavered. He kept reminding us daily that, "Since we have nothing better — this has got to be the best."

Like everything else, nothing comes to stay; it all comes to pass. One day the war was over. We had survived. We celebrated the day by using up the last bits of hoarded foods, unconcerned about the next day. After all, we were free. My father always said the world belongs to the free — they can accomplish anything. There was food the next day. He was right, of course. The heat became bearable, the food edible, and the future took on shape and form.

Soon the heartbreaking news from a war-torn Europe reached us. We learned of the terrible death camps, the atrocities, and faced the tragic loss of friends and families. We mourned the millions of faceless victims who died in horror — at the whim and will of a madman's nightmare.

All of us had moments of guilt for having survived the Holocaust; these reflections could not dampen the unquenchable joy we felt for being alive. I'm sure each one of us made a solemn promise to do his part to prevent mass murder from ever happening again. We had been spared; we would make something of our lives; we had to live for those who had died.

It would be two years before we emigrated to America, and during that time I lied about my age and went to work for the United States Army in China as a local civil servant. (That was the last time I added years to my age. I've been going in the opposite direction ever since.) Clerical positions were bountiful, and applicants could choose a job with the branch of service that promised to be the most interesting or the least complicated.

I landed a job with the China Theater Replacement Center in Shanghai, which turned out to be a hoot and a holler and a scratch behind the ears! A few months later, I was transferred to Nanking's MAGIC command (Military Advisory Group in China). And magic it was, and more magic was needed but never arrived. Hence, the country became the Republic of China and the Red Star waved.

According to my bosses, both in Shanghai and Nanking, things at U.S. Army headquarters ran their true course and were definitely SNAFU — situation normal, all fouled up. Young officers who knew all about football, comic strips and war found themselves assigned to supervisory positions without a clue of what to do. Memos and general orders flew around our command like confetti at a New Year's party, only to be swept up with the rest of the remnants of the festivities. Baby-faced enlisted men held down jobs that defied description but seemed to be a barrel of fun. Desks were used to rest one's feet, and the soles of shoes were the first thing one faced upon entering an office. Colonels and general excepted — they were playing golf and kept the soles of their shoes firmly attached to the greens.

Uncle Sam's army had won the war, and to hell with the paperwork!

But what about those diplomatic dinners entertaining a string of imposing guests of honor? And what about those making-friendly cocktail affairs to cement international relationships — in spite of their dubious beginnings? What about protocol? And how do you spell p-r-o-t-o-c-o-l? And who's in charge?

To the young officers and attachés — first time away from home — social, military and diplomatic protocol, seating arrangements, menu selections, and general decorum for entertaining in a foreign land were giant puzzles. No one beneath the rank of a general or a colonel gave a hoot about protocol or cared on which side of the plate the salad fork belonged.

These lackadaisical heroes had only recently fought their way through the blood-soaked battlefields of the China-Burma-India Theater of War and lived to tell about it. They were celebrating life itself. A party meant a drink in one hand, their feet propped on a table, and a never-ending flow of do-you-remember … Guam … Okinawa … Leyte … Corregidor … Taratuga … Colonel Mudface … Major Kaka-Doodledoo … Second-Louie Sweet Face … Sergeant Son-of-a-Bitch … Private Hangover-Kosowski … Were you at Iwo Jima … Remember Spam with chocolate syrup on Christmas Day … candy bars with jungle rot … Long-legged Layover Lily … Pock-faced Polly Phew … soggy graham crackers … letters from home … no letters from home … rain, swamps, mosquitoes the size of a Texas bat … snipers and more jungle rot … Do you remember? Were you there?

The men were not interested in overseeing official dinners; they were too busy reliving the glory and the muck of a long, wretched campaign, making up for lost time and speculating on an uncertain future … going home! The War Was Over.

Attending an official dinner party one night with one of the officers for whom I worked, I almost ended up under the table trying to control my hysterical fits of laughter at the goings-on at the table. Captain B. (he was from Atlanta and hard to understand) turned to me during one of my more sober moments and directed me sternly to: "Don't just sit there and howl, young lady — do something — y'all!" I agreed.

Having grown up among adults and, come to think of it, having been treated like one (lots of responsibility and little fun!), I had watched "how things were done." I had observed people in all sorts of situations handle themselves with grace, social savvy and admirable control. And then there was always my esteemed friend, the good Lady Constanza.

I was not in awe of a seating chart. All it took for me to provide a welcome but sophisticated setting for a VIP was to give some thought to his nationality, his professional and social status, plus whatever gossip I could glean about the individual's personality and habits from talkative staff and chatty house servants. Easy. I spoke a few languages and could prattle some street talk in the local Chinese dialect.

Instinctively, and with surprisingly few mistakes for someone of my tender years, I managed to conquer the touchy seating arrangements for harmonious diplomatic gatherings, as well as prevent catastrophic culinary results from those self-appointed Chinese comedians who ran the kitchens and caused a ton of mayhem.

It wasn't difficult to get to the bottom of the problems in the kitchen. Born pranksters, artistically inclined and sexually shameless, the Chinese have delighted in openly embarrassing the tight-laced foreigners about intimate matters from the day the first missionary set foot on China's soil. The cooks who found employment at American embassies, consulates, and service clubs for the military howled with glee and snickered themselves silly while arranging mashed potatoes on a dinner plate, carefully sculpting the soft mass to resemble women's breasts. These jokers would top each mound with a ripe-red maraschino cherry in a shimmering circle of hot-pink cherry juice.

Desserts were another matter and offered the cooks endless opportunities for creating biologically-inspired sculptures. One of the favorite desserts was the good old American banana split, which lent itself to a variety of designs.

An arrangement of two well-formed scoops of vanilla ice cream resting snugly on either side of a large banana — a coffee bean strategically embedded at one end — the ice cream cleverly sprinkled with finely shredded bits of chocolate-dipped coconut, was placed in front of each hot-faced guest for dessert. Accompanied by hoots of laughter and piercing shrieks of uncontrolled hysteria, the waiters literally danced out of the dining rooms on their velvet-clad feet and left for the next province — at least overnight.

The diplomatic corps couldn't handle that kind of hurrah more than once. And, considering the wealth of Chinese artistic talents and their overactive fascination with sex, there would be no end to sculpting food into erotic displays at mealtime.

Six years of growing up on the streets of Shanghai, drinking tea from delicate bowls with hand-painted scenes from the *Kama Sutra* hiding beneath green tea leaves, hearing eight-year-old boy pimps touting the astonishing sexual talents of their nine-year-old sisters in sing-song Pidgin English, had left me with an interesting, if not unorthodox, form of sex education. No doubt Nanny and my parents would have had a fit had they learned how I came about such explicit carnal knowledge, which originated solely from the seamy, steamy side of Shanghai street life.

Karma was on my side. The cooks came to understand quickly that their days of fun at the expense of the "devil foreigners" would have to come to a dead stop. This "young missie" who brooked no deviation from proper food arrangements on the plates would see them sliced and pickled in Buddha's hell and roasted over dragon fires if they disobeyed. They were impressed by my eloquent string of treasured Chinese curses unrivaled in any other language — it's almost pure poetry.

I had no problem issuing strict instructions accompanied by an endless barrage of horrible threats concerning food presentation to a number of giggly, local culinary quacks. Mashed potatoes, vegetables, meat portions and a variety of desserts soon looked as respectable and innocuous as those served at an Iowa church picnic at harvest time.

Helping to arrange diplomatic dinners made me realize how important it was to seat the "right" people next to each other or across from each other. I also relied heavily on the "diplomatic" training — in civilian life we call it good manners — people had received. I hoped fervently that, if seated incorrectly, that person would be "diplomatic" enough not to start World War III. I also discovered if I seated a difficult person next to another difficult person, and they didn't have the use of a common language for conversing, no harm would be done. The two dinner partners would toast each other solemnly, then nod and smile, and smile and nod all the way through to the demitasse, with the result that world peace was preserved until the next state dinner.

I learned a valuable lesson: It doesn't take a genius to figure out that if you bring the right people together the success rate for a good time is assured. However, that does not mean that a bit of controversy, a different approach to the same subject, or an outrageous view on a "holy-cow" subject is not welcome. *Au contraire!* People love a lively but well-mannered controversy — the mischievous villain — as long as humor overrides, and a good-natured, civilized exchange of ideas is possible. And the hostess, according to my British expert, the good Lady Constanza, controls the situation.

Our days in China came to an end after eight and a half years. Communist armies were overrunning the country, and the stateless European refugees were eager to find a new home — a real home, a place of permanence. A few of the people we had shared our life with returned to Europe, some went to Palestine — soon to become Israel, a handful ventured to Australia and New Zealand, but the majority went "home" to the United States.

The moment I set foot on American soil, walked the streets of San Francisco, felt the heartbeat of this young nation, breathed the free air, I knew I had indeed come home. Our little family settled in Denver, where I started my new life with a young husband, a picket fence, kids, PTA, spring cleaning, *Oklahoma!, The Sound of Music,* green lawns without dandelions, paper towels, clean water, crabgrass, Gold Bond Stamps, a friendly dog, measles, ice cream, grapes, fresh eggs, green vegetables, and jars of mayonnaise!

Once we were settled in, on weekends I played my favorite game of "guess who's coming to dinner." I cooked and baked, experimented with recipes, tried out new things, found inexpensive ways to create table settings on dimestore money, and slowly created ME — my own style.

My mother used to say that it was to my advantage to have been born in Germany, raised in China and able to "mature" in America. (I felt like a bottle of wine that improved with age and rotation.) She insisted that my having had the benefit of a three-continent upbringing "rounded me out" — at least I would know enough about people and manners to be a good hostess — if nothing else. Mother may have preferred me to be a real true-blue Martha Perfect — some mothers are like that — but that was too much to ask from someone like me who'd rather shoot from the hip even if I hit my foot occasionally.

Of course, you don't have to be perfect to create a memorable evening for your friends and yourself. Just relax, adopt a good measure of that "what-the-hell attitude," be selective in your choice of dinner partners, prepare most of the meal ahead of time, set your table and pick up your house a day or two before the event. Fill your rooms with fresh flowers — cut or in pots — light a few candles, play soft music, and keep it simple. Get out of the kitchen and join your guests — that's the sign of a clever hostess. Then you can sit back, gloat a little as you survey your handiwork, and watch the evening come to life.

All you have to remember is that you're NOT competing with somebody's dressed-up game hen doing handstands on a bed of pickled moss. You're doing things your way — plan well, prepare ahead, keep it simple, and enjoy yourself. I promise you'll have fun. The magic works every time!

Chapter Three

How to Stage, Direct and Star at Your Own Party

The only real stumbling block is fear of failure.
In cooking you've got to have a what-the-hell attitude.

– Julia Child

The above mentioned what-the-hell attitude is not just for cooking; it is also useful if applied in large doses to the matter of entertaining. You'll see what I mean.

I know women (don't you?) who subscribe to every food magazine, read the latest culinary guides, own a handsome collection of cookbooks, and have built a shrine to Julia Child. They have abandoned curling up with a steamy romance or a page-turner mystery in preference to going to bed with a cookbook. They slip between the covers clutching a year's supply of the latest in gourmet literature, which they voraciously devour and annotate — potboiler or not. I know people who lose weight when they stop reading cookbooks. Really!

In real life, these *bon gourmet* fanatics are closet fast-food junkies and eat over the sink.

I know women who reign over an Aladdin's palace of gadgetry and widgetry. They own every kind of masher, mixer and mincer, beater and blender, shredder and slicer, sieve and sifter, grater and grinder. They can lay their hands on every non-stick pot, poacher, pan and skillet. They even have an English-speaking wok.

In real life, they rarely cook.

I know women who, ever since their wedding day have hidden their china, silver and crystal, along with their snowy linens, in the dusty recesses of attics, basements, and under the stairs.

In real life, they don't set a table. They use paper plates.

I know women who live in lovely, spacious homes with manicured gardens straight from the slick pages of *Better Living.* Their dining room tables, which are polished to a high sheen and seat eight people comfortably, are virgin territory and remain a wasteland where not even dust dares to gather. The living room is tastefully furnished, begging to be occupied. The house is a showcase for Johnson's Wax, Drexel furniture, and is a realtor's dream.

They don't entertain, either.

Things are not quite perfect for them. They plan to stencil their driveway and wait for the wooden trellis to bloom — maybe next year.

I also know women who spend large amounts of money on eating out but claim that entertaining is too expensive.

Several of these reluctant hostesses speak enviously of mothers and friends who are great cooks, who know how to stretch time and a penny, who can throw a dinner party at the drop of wooden spoon with their hands tied behind their backs, and are s-o-o-o-o organized. These self-appointed victims constantly voice their desire to be able to entertain. They moan how they yearn to reciprocate the generous acts of hospitality extended to them, and pine to get into the swing of socializing, if only they knew how.

Time and time again, I've had friends and acquaintances confess to me sheepishly that, if only they could "DO" as well as I, they would; if only they weren't petrified of … this, that or the other; if only there were more time, more money, no children, better weather, and Mars got out of retrograde. They keep insisting that they would just l-o-o-v-e to entertain but…. Well, enough excuses.

All the nervous hostess has to do in order to have some fun is to jump over her own shadow, grow an herb garden along with some confidence, and decide to make it happen. It has been my experience that, with a little effort, anything can be learned.

Here's what's the matter:
- Having time is a matter of choice.
- Making time is a matter of discipline and organization.
- Entertaining is not a matter of money or gourmet cookery, but it is a matter of style, taste and thought.
- Food is not nearly as memorable as the people who grace your table, and the atmosphere you, the hostess, conjure up.

All it takes is determination, confidence, a bit of work and some planning to set the stage for a lovely evening. I have made my own rules with which I approach the matter of entertaining, and which, if you choose to follow, will most certainly set you on the road to hostessing fun:

Plan Your Meals to Fit Your Budget

A festive and elegant meal does not have to cost a fortune. It doesn't require endless hours of kitchen gastronomics, a degree in home economics, or a seven-year residency with the Martha Perfect Shacks and Swamps Institute. Remember her? She's the one who made a decoupaged collage out of onion skins and garlic peelings for her loving-hands-at-home dissertation.

But let's go back to the real world.

In the last twenty-five years, food magazines have been challenging us "ordinary" people to pit our skills, endurance, and our pocketbooks against the top chefs, who are making culinary history in their ivory-tower kitchens in Paris, Rome and New York. These epicurean stars think nothing of paying a king's ransom for a handful of truffles. Without blinking an eye, chefs order pounds of beluga caviar at fifty dollars an ounce for an impressive hors d'oeuvre. They even fly in a cluster of fresh Maine lobsters on their very own private jet. Chefs are able (and get paid) to spend endless hours fussing over a dish and to employ several nimble assistants who do the rest of the work. I don't know a chef who has to clean house, take the kids to baseball practice, ballet or bungee-jumping lessons, or has ever done the laundry in between stuffing baby squabs. Shucks!

None of the above is necessary. At this writing, it is still possible to serve a delicious dinner for six to eight, including nibbles and dessert, for around thirty dollars.

(Add to that a bottle or two of wine.) Try to beat that cost in a restaurant. It can't be done — not even at the *Golden Doors Drive-Out.*

I only give in to buying expensive temptations at special markets and fancy culinary pleasure domes if I've won three scratch tickets in a row, and the return on my bottle count was high. Most of the time I shop within my budget.

Here are some points to ponder and budgets to be rescued:

Don't buy out-of-season asparagus (or any other kind of produce) at five dollars a pound — serve frozen snap peas instead. They too are green, aren't they? It's pure silliness to purchase Arava melon at ten dollars apiece, or feel compelled to serve a bottle of wine that someone decorated with a forty-dollar price tag. Why buy Napoleon brandy? The old boy's been dead for a long time, and you can't possibly hurt his feelings if you serve an affordable label.

If the recipe calls for marscapone and you cringe at the price tag, use large-curd cottage cheese at one-fourth the cost. Place the cottage cheese in a high-speed blender until silky-smooth and add a teaspoon of sugar — *voilà:* marscapone.

A good recipe (see recipe section) for Jewish chicken-liver pâté is economical, tasty and easier to pronounce than *Strassbourg foie de gras avec truffles.* A few chopped black olives — the frugal cook's answer to the black-truffles effect — may be an act of deception, but no one has ever asked me: "Is this a truffle, my dear, or is it perchance merely a lowly minced black olive?" Personally, I often wonder if that truffle isn't a fly in the ointment. It certainly looks like one!

If your pocketbook screams at the cost of beef fillet or a fancy crown roast of lamb, switch to a more affordable menu. Remember, fillets and crown roasts demand last-minute precision-type attention and can easily be turned into shoe leather by the late arrival of a guest. Switch gears, prepare something that is economical and doesn't self-destruct in case dinner is delayed. That kind of financial strategy may just buy the flowers for your table or pay for a babysitter to keep the little darlings out of your hair.

When you make your budget for an evening of entertaining, establish what you want to achieve, list your options and your priorities. Remember: "If you have two loaves of bread, sell one and buy a lily."

When a recipe calls for a bit of chopped, fresh this-or-that-herb and the market price is prohibitive, substitute dried herbs. It's quite all right; only the ghost of Escoffier himself would detect the difference, and he isn't invited, is he? Or, if you have the inclination, grow your own herbs in a windowsill garden in your kitchen — right along with a batch of what-the-hell attitude à la Julia.

Do you recall that recipe you so sneakily tore out of a magazine at the dentist's office when no one was looking? That delicious-sounding *Scallopini Napoleonese* that required a whole bunch of imported mushrooms with a long name straight from the secret gardens at the edge of Mt. Vesuvius? Don't fret it! You can substitute good old American button mushrooms. It doesn't make that much difference in the flavor or texture of a dish. An old teacher of mine once told me: "Mushrooms are all the same; just the poisonous ones are different!" Soothing advice if ever I heard.

Another purchase that can dip one's budget quickly into the red herring level is maintaining a supply of a variety of exotic and costly liqueurs for cooking. Framboise, Calvados and other brews with outrageous names rarely come in pint-sized bottles. You can spend a small fortune on a fifth of that imported stuff. I have discovered that a modest American applejack does right well against a French Calvados, and an inexpensive Triple Sec replaces the highbrow Framboise in my kitchen. I like Triple Sec because it delivers a pleasant, fruity flavor and does the job.

The chef-type food aficionados, no doubt, will turn up their noses at such plebeian recommendations and may argue passionately that the delicate flavors of fine alcoholic brews are responsible for that distinct difference between merely good food and fine gourmet morsels. Dyed-in-the-wool gourmet cooks may be mortally wounded by these suggested substitutions and heave their non-stick, copper crêpe pans at me. So be it. I'll duck!

I truly believe that food is only one aspect of a party — your guests, the setting you provide, the sparkle of good conversation — make the occasion an event. Oops, here I've said it again.

In an interview for a magazine article, a reporter once asked Abigail Van Buren about her favorite foods and the most fabulous meal she ever had. The famous author replied: 'I don't remember the name of the restaurant, I can't recall what I ate, but the company was divine; it was unforgettable."

That's what entertaining is all about. Even at a leisurely pace, a meal is consumed in little more than one hour. Those sixty-plus minutes represent only a fragment of the time your guests spend in your home. No one will remember if indeed the mushrooms were *portobello al capone* and the *zabaglione* was made with real Framboise. But your guests will remember the magic of the occasion, and you will cherish the afterglow of a wonderful evening until the next one and the next one.

You won't find recipes in this book whose ingredients have to be purchased at "specialty stores." You won't be burdened with tricky seven-starred dishes that demand an endless list of ingredients, or foods that require twenty or more steps of preparation. I won't use a recipe that needs as much time to complete as my Aunt Ami's five-hundred-piece jigsaw puzzle. Life's too short to stuff mushrooms.

If my budget can't handle a gourmet cut of meat (or that Maine lobster with a caviar necktie) plus the cost of fresh flowers — I always opt for a big bunch of posies and gladly change my menu to something that keeps me within my budget. If I planned to serve bouillabaisse preceded by my favorite hot appetizer — fresh crab and artichoke dip (see recipe section) — but the price of seafood has gone over the sea wall and beyond on that particular day — I switch to pasta with clam sauce and serve a plain artichoke dip. I will still be offering delicious food, but it will be easy on the budget.

The menus in the recipe section are based on current market costs in the Pacific Northwest. There may be variations in food prices, especially fresh fruits and vegetables, in other parts of the country. In that case, look for compatible substitute produce available at a more reasonable price.

There is absolutely nothing wrong with serving chicken and less expensive cuts of meat. It all depends on how food is prepared. (You'll find some absolutely delicious chicken menus in the recipe section.) The reputation of a dish lies in its flavor, texture, and the way it is presented. Pasta dishes with savory sauces and colorful ingredients are economical and healthy and can look positively mouth-watering.

Living in the Pacific Northwest is somewhat advantageous as far as the economics and availability of seafood, fresh fruit and vegetables are concerned. Even though I sometimes think there's no substitute for salmon, the sauces and condiments listed in the recipe section also enhance the flavor of what some refer to as the less-distinguished creatures of the ocean. I do it all the time — no complaints.

So you see, an elegant and festive meal does not ever have to cost a fortune.

Sure, it would be nice to have help around the house before, in between and after a dinner party — just ask Martha Perfect; she has lots of help all the time. However, if you start organizing and prioritizing your activities, implementing effective shortcuts, and do not leave things to the last minute, you will be surprised how smoothly things can go — without help.

Any dish I can't prepare in thirty minutes, I don't fool with. I still run a house and my work and have set a limit to the time I take out of a busy day to plan and prepare for a dinner party. On average, it takes me no more than two hours to get it all done — that includes preparing the main dish and dessert ahead of time, as well as setting the table.

Let me tell you how I work — perhaps it will get you going, too:

After I have invited my guests and confirmed the date and time, I plan the menu and the setting — keeping in mind the season.

Day Two Before the Dinner Party

1. I check my larder, pantry, refrigerator and freezer to see that everything I need for the menu I intend to serve is in the house.

2. If I don't plan to use the dessert I still have on hand in the freezer for whatever reason (maybe I served it to the same guests at our last get-together), I make a different dessert at this time.

3. I threaten my family with being left out of my will if anyone so much as just thinks about "checking on the dessert to make sure it honors the occasion." I am not taken in by the innocent remark, "Oh, gee whiz, just looking!"

4. I make sure that the linens I plan to use are clean and ironed, and that I have the right kind of candles in my secret cache. To be on the safe side, I keep all sizes and colors on hand, plus white candles, — after all, white (just like diamonds) goes with everything.

Day One Before the Dinner Party

1. I get the house ready, and paint a dim future for my husband and children should they decide to build a paper-mâché horse in the living room — or anywhere else on the premises, for that matter. I have also learned to watch for signs that my dearly beloved yearns to bring the model railroad up from the basement and set it up on the dining room table. But you already knew that!

2. I set my table — all but the fresh flowers.

3. I line up the dinner plates I plan to use on my kitchen counter.

4. I shop for flowers.

5. If the recipe I plan to use calls for chopped parsley, grated orange or lemon zest, I do it that day and store it in small bowls tightly covered with clear wrap.

6.   I cook all those "prepare-ahead" dishes and store according to directions
7.   Most of the work is done.

Day of the Dinner Party

1.   Since I've done almost all the chores ahead of time, I don't give dinner another thought until it's time to:
   • Remove prepared food from refrigerator or freezer — bring to room temperature.
   • Fix pre-dinner nibbles.
   • Rescue the flowers from the refrigerator and arrange them.
   • Put the finishing touches on the meal.
   • Place a stack of CDs in the music box.
   • Get dressed and wait for the arrival of my friends.
   Just do it! It just takes a little practice. Try it; you might like it!

Chapter Four

Preparing for Your Dinner Party

Try to avoid snobbism. Cooking is not for showing off to the neighbors.
— French Chef Jacques Pepin

Over the years I have met a lot of excellent cooks. They have attended gourmet cooking classes and have made cooking a serious hobby. These clever at-home chefs delight in gastronomic gymnastics. Their meals do back flips, and the dessert is no less daring and complicated than a high-wire act without a net. These cookery wizards have the stamina and courage to concoct a last-minute sauce consisting of at least twenty-two ingredients, eleven steps of preparation, and a generous splashing of Remy Martin, worth a king's ransom — followed by that dreadful threat: Serve immediately!

She spends hours in preparation for the meal, and the moment her guests arrive she disappears into her kitchen, where she spends a good part of the evening while her friends do their own thing in the living room. Now you see her, now you don't!

I have great admiration for the hostess and her five-star gourmet dinners — but that's not for me. My hobby may be cooking, but my passion is people, and I want to spend as much time with my guests as I can squeeze out of an evening. And that means not spending my time in the kitchen.

Then there is another kind of entertaining where everyone pitches in and helps prepare the meal and bring it to the table.

Magazines are full of those chic everybody-digs-in-and-helps-cook kitchen parties wrapped in a cloud of clever chatter about this, that and nothing else. I don't do that either. I'm just not that chic. The one time I tried it, I had a triple accident. My chilled, crisp green salad wilted to death when an eager helper rinsed the greens in hot water and preheated the salad plates. Someone else mistook the cayenne pepper for paprika, and the caramelized onion-mushroom sauté was so "hot" it caused first-degree palate burns and ate a hole in the garbage disposal. Another eager volunteer poured the steamed clams — juice, sand, *bouquet garni* and all — in the ready-to-serve bouillabaisse. Try to explain that one away! I truly believe that too many cooks do spoil a whole lot of good food.

I have developed — as you can if you give yourself a chance — my own shortcuts and ways for the quickest way to get dinner cooked and served and myself out of the kitchen.

The number one rule you will read more than once in this book is:

Keep It Simple and Plan Ahead to Avoid Last-Minute Disasters.

There is absolutely no reason to impress your guests by serving them *Poulet Magnifique* clad in a clever checkerboard puff pastry nightie, surrounded by Spanish kumquats, hand-dipped in *Glacé Champs Elysée.* Just what have you accomplished? You can bathe for a second or so in your guests' enthusiastic applause, their awe, and the heart-flattering sounds of ohhhs and ahhhs — just before you pass out. So? After all that work, you'll be exhausted and will want to don your old purple robe, draw the shades, and go to bed with a head-pounding migraine.

What if, as you slice into your *Poulet Magnifique,* you discover the never-fail puff pastry has turned to clay and you'll need a hammer and chisel to get to the meat. Horrors upon horrors. The twice-baked chicken has turned into a fowl fossil and is drier than a popcorn ball on a desert floor. It happens, you know. Many of those high-flying recipes are no different than the latest collection of Paris clothes featured in *La Belle Mode* — "Looks great on paper; just don't try to wear it (or eat it)."

Stick to the things you have learned to prepare with confidence. Get a handle on it and create ways to present your offerings in an appealing fashion. Just don't over-do!

Today's trendy chefs decorate a dinner plate with anything from zig-zags of roasted red-pepper purée, wild swirls of "sauce unknown," to a generous dusting of parsley ground to a powder-like substance. (If this would have happened in the days of my father, I can just imagine his caustic request: "Take this back into the kitchen, please, and bring me a clean plate.") By the by, pepper berries on simply everything is "in." But you read that in *W,* didn't you?

Julia Child commented on super-doer decorated dishes with a caustic, "It's so beautifully arranged on the plate — you know someone's fingers have been all over it."

In other words, don't try to outdo the outdoers — they get paid for it; you don't.

Follow these suggestions for preparing a meal, and you will save time and nerves.

1. Always begin your preparations in a clean kitchen with a clean sink — clear the deck for action.

2. Start the evening of your party with an empty dishwasher. There is no bigger nuisance than to be ready to put your dinner dishes away and find the dishwasher loaded — clean or dirty, it makes no difference. It will delay your clean-up and add a chore you could have done before.

3. Cook ahead as many parts of your menu plan as possible.

4. As you use bowls, spoons, skillets, measuring cups, saucepans and other utensils, wash and dry them as soon as they've served their purpose. Everything is then ready to be put away, or to be used for the next thing you want to prepare. Do not let utensils clutter up your sink and counter space.

5. If you have a spill, especially on your stove top or floor, clean it up at once. Don't wait until you're "all done."

6. Familiarize yourself with the recipe you have chosen. Measure and line up all ingredients on your kitchen counter in the order they are to be used. (I use inexpensive clear glass bowls for no-mistake cooking.) Return all condiments and spices to their storage place. Keep the counter clear.

7. For tearless handling, chill onions in the refrigerator before using, and instead of chopping them by hand, use your food processor or handy mincer. It saves time and tears.

8. Use kitchen shears coated with cooking spray for cutting dried fruit. Use shears to trim fat from poultry and meat. Unless you have a sharp butcher knife, try using the shears for cutting meat into strips — it works for me.
9. Keep a pair of small pliers on hand for pulling bones out of salmon fillets before broiling or baking.
10. Alphabetize your collection of herbs and spices.
11. Keep all your refrigerated condiments in a large container, such as a deep plastic dishpan. It eliminates hunting for that tiny jar of hot mustard or garlic pesto among the scattered contents of your refrigerator.
12. Keep your oils, vinegars and prepared sauces in one place.
13. Use prepared condiments to save time and prevent your kitchen from turning into a disaster zone. (Let somebody else grind, chop and grate!)

Keep on hand:

Prepared crushed garlic
Prepared minced ginger
Pesto (several kinds)
Whole or chopped green peppers
Roasted red peppers, whole
Roasted red peppers, chopped
Several kinds of prepared mustards (Dijon, stone
    ground, hot and sweet and regular)
Small cans of chopped olives
A variety of chutneys
Prepared marinara sauce
Sun-dried tomatoes packed in olive oil

Packages of Hollandaise and Bearnaise sauces *(Knorr*
    sauce base), which I doctor up. (See recipe section.)
Several packages of dried onion soup
Several kinds of vinegars that bring a variety of
    flavors to salads.

Make your own list of things you use often and keep
them on hand. (When I shop, I always buy two of everything. It's the hoarder in me.)

Keep cans of chicken and beef stock chilled for
several hours before using. The fat settles in lumps, which
can be easily discarded; or buy fat-free, low-sodium brands.

After years of planning dinners and reading a ton of
cookbooks and gourmet magazines, I am able to look a
recipe in the eye and determine at a glance if it is good, very
good or awful. I can forecast the flavor of the dish by the
kind and quantities of recommended ingredients. I won't
touch a recipe that calls for a can of mushroom soup, or so-
called helpers, stuffers and fillers. Things like that can ruin
the natural flavor of the dish.

Too much salt and too much pepper are not only bad
habits, but they over-kill the delicate blends and balance of
the other ingredients. I rarely use salt in my cooking. I keep
salt cellars on the table for guests to help themselves.
However, I usually remove the little containers from the
dinner table untouched.

The number of ingredients and steps listed for
preparing something has a lot to do with whether or not I
will ever try a recipe — even if the full-color picture
literally jumps on my plate. Culinary somersaults are a lost
cause as far as I am concerned — that's time spent I don't
have, and the results are most often not worth the effort.

I tried out a new-to-me dessert recipe which promised
to be relatively simple to prepare, with only a limited

number of ingredients. However, by the time I had followed the step-by-step instructions and baked the dessert, my sink looked as if I had cooked for a Kansas county fair — no kidding! I had used the following utensils all at the same time, which now needed to be washed and put away:

Four measuring cups (all I own) — four mixing bowls — two small glass bowls — one juicer — one blender — one electric mixer — two rubber scrapers — three wooden spoons — one paring knife — one plastic bowl with lid — one bundt pan — one large Pyrex dish — one cooling rack — and that blasted partridge in a pear tree!

That's half my kitchen!

I have to admit, the Lemon Baba (see recipe section) is worth the effort, but it's not something you want to do if you're pushed for time, don't own four measuring cups, and prefer skydiving to dessert making.

As you begin — or revive — your hostess career, tackle only those dinners for which at least two-thirds of the meal is prepared a day — or more — ahead. It also helps if some of your dishes can be completed in the morning and put on hold until evening. Avoid critical last-minute treatments to a dish. When a recipe demands: "… and serve immediately" — stay away. Stay far away! To me that means "do it before it dies." Life's too short to grill a silver sole for exactly seven split seconds on a bed of mermaid tears, mist with barrel-aged basil dew — and serve — immediately! That's enough to turn me on to a diet of bread and water.

Do last-minute-crucial-to-the-outcome tricks to no more than *one* part of the meal, and do that only when it won't make a nervous wreck out of you, and you are cooking with your newly acquired what-the-hell confidence firmly in place. Shredded cabbage is fine; shredded nerves are awful.

That same "don't do" applies to experimenting with a new (untried-by-you) recipe the day of your dinner party. Robert Carrier, a New York chef and famous restaurateur, advises, "When entertaining, make only dishes which you know. Try out anything new on the cat."

If you don't have a cat, have a dress rehearsal for a new menu with your family. Kids, however, may act like cats and turn up their noses at anything new, or disappear into their rooms, where they've stashed a tired hamburger or two.

When planning your menu, think of how things taste, and visualize how the main course will look when all the components are on one plate. If, for instance, you have used a lot of pesto with your pasta, leave it off the chicken and the salad. Introduce a different flavor to prevent things from tasting alike so that they can complement each other. If you cook everything you serve with a lot of garlic — well, garlic is about all you're going to taste.

Use foods of contrasting colors: don't serve sliced tomatoes or red beets alongside a marinara sauce. If you have made a spinach filling for crêpes or cannelloni, avoid serving another green vegetable. In other words, paint a picture with the food you serve — create contrast and make it look appealing.

If you serve dinner from the kitchen on individual plates, be creative. Add a touch of green, a sprig of fennel or thyme, a twist or wedge of citrus fruit, a slice or two of kiwi, curls of raw carrots. Sprinkle mashed potatoes or rice with a dash of paprika or finely grated parsley and place your offering on a dark green, frizzy leaf of collard greens. (Kale and savoy cabbage make great display enhancers.) Again, make it pretty. Prepare your *"garni"* ahead of time, line up the dinner plates, and have a plan in which order you serve what, and how you present it. Do not get complicated; keep it simple.

An artist friend of mine dreamt that for three days she carved a hundred tiny jack-o-lanterns from carrot tops, strung them on a strand of angel hair pasta, and dropped her creations in individual bowls filled with a polka-dot cream of pumpkin soup. She woke up in the dead of night, panicky, and decided right there to delay her next dinner party. She was going to use the flimsy excuse of having to carve a hundred miniature jack-o-lanterns for her menu. Some people will do anything to get out of entertaining.

All this silly story proves is that there is a limit to being creative and artistic — especially if your prize chef just eloped with your kitchen maid, and you're It. It's fun to create a lovely meal, but it can be ever so simple. Let Martha Perfect and her staff of eighty do her New England Luau and Menehuni Flambé — it's too much for me.

Here is a simple thing you can do that gives your salad a different look and will surprise your guests. Soak a head of cabbage (red or green) in warm water for two hours. Remove and shake off excess water. With a sharp paring knife, remove two or more inches of the core, which helps release the cabbage leaves. Carefully peel away the larger outer leaves and fill each with individual portions of a tossed green salad, cucumber or polka-dot salad (see recipe section). Place the cabbage "bowl" on a decorative plate. If necessary, balance it with a wedge of lemon or tomato so it won't keel over, and serve. Your guests will be delighted, and it hasn't cost you more than five minutes of your time.

Use a variety of readily available salad greens (wild greens are delicious and colorful) and decorate with one or two pansies (no plastic or silk blossoms, please) for that well-deserved ooohhh and aaahhh of appreciation your creation will command. Top "just greens" with four to six stalks of asparagus "tied" with a strip of roasted red pepper. I prepare my asparagus "bundles " ahead of time, place them on a plate, sprinkle them with a dash of rice or balsamic vinegar, cover them with clear plastic wrap, and refrigerate until dinnertime. (It takes five minutes to create six asparagus bundles. (See recipe section.)

For a different look and taste, prepare a medley of pickled mushrooms, fresh or canned julienned pears, and chopped pecans for a salad topper. Use a fruity and light-hearted vinaigrette on the greens. There is a variety of clever and appealing ways to serve green salads, fruit salads and soups in all kinds of natural containers. You can hollow out mini pumpkins, acorn squash or cannonball breads to serve as soup bowls *au naturelle.*

You can make baskets by removing the meat from an orange or grapefruit and filling the shells with fruit salad. You can hollow out melons of all kinds and sizes to become serving pieces and bowls. They can be carved in such a way that they even have lids and handles. Clever, clever!

You can do that if you have the time and endless patience. But then, you've seen that featured in all those smart "Modern Mansions & Sunken Gardens" magazines. Martha Perfect's nimble little fingers do it all the time — ever so adroitly. She can do anything as long as she keeps a big smile on her face and a pair of Wellingtons on her feet as she leans against a weathered barn door. So picturesque! She never has her photo taken with her staff of eighty "assistants."

All kidding aside, all you want to do is choose good ingredients and plan your combination of the meat or fish portions of your dinner in harmony with the side dishes for color and taste. Then arrange each part of the meal in an attractive fashion on your lovely dishes ... and serve ... whenever you're ready!

While you are practicing becoming an effective hostess in both the kitchen and the living room, create a system, a method, by which to operate. Find your own shortcuts for saving motion and time. Invest a little time and do a dress rehearsal with your dinner and salad dishes and come up with your own time savers. If you have generous counter space in your kitchen, prepare the area for quick and efficient serving. If you have little space, just stack your dinner dishes within easy access to the food.

On a spot — next to your surface unit or stove — line up your dinner plates, serving utensils and garnishes for quick handling. Prepare two plates at a time and serve. Remember, serve from the left, remove from the right. That's if you really, really care — but you don't have to. Prepare small to medium-sized portions; cover pots and pans to keep food warm to fill second-helping requests.

Do not overload a plate with food. Dress it up a bit. Presentation is important. Make it look appealing and appetizing, and don't overwhelm your guests with large quantities. If they can't eat it all, you might think they didn't like it — you feel bad, and the evening is ruined, and, and....

If you have prepared a dessert in individual glasses (See recipe section for lemon and chocolate mousse), take them out of the refrigerator just before you serve dinner. Place the dessert on a tray and cover with a clean piece of linen or a kitchen towel, so guests can't peek. If you plan to use individual decorative plates for serving, have them ready. As soon as you've cleared the table after dinner, it takes but a moment to uncover the dessert and serve from your place at the table — quick and smooth. Everybody will think you're a magician. You can do that kind of magic; all it takes is strategy and preparation!

Practice makes for a good hostess. You'll be surprised how quickly you can become adept at giving dinner parties — especially when you treat the matter as if you had done it all your life. Be casual, be cool!

Summary: Do's and Don'ts

Change your mind — your attitude — about cooking *Remember the number one priority:* Invite people you like and respect, and who share common ground. Don't invite people *you owe* — take them to lunch!

❦ ❦ ❦

1. Cooking is a gracious, warm and nurturing kind of thing to offer people. For someone like me, cooking is therapy. It is totally relaxing, absorbing, and a great outlet for stored-up energy. It's creative; it's giving. (author unknown)

2. Always keep your pantry, your freezer and refrigerator well stocked so you can rise to the occasion.

3. Ask first-time guests if they have food allergies, h-a-t-e broccoli, or have special dietary requirements — it eliminates unpleasant surprises.

4. Do plan your menu for balance: flavors, texture, contrast in color, season and availability on the market.

5. Don't be ambitious and serve an eight-course dinner to impress your friends. Do not spend your life in the kitchen. It is totally unnecessary and may turn you off forever from entertaining.

6.   Don't plan a meal that threatens to "go bad" or die if the dinner hour is delayed.

7.   Do start with a clean kitchen, wash utensils immediately, and use them for the next thing you prepare.

8.   Don't overload individual servings — offer seconds.

9.   Do keep foods covered and warm for serving seconds.

10.   Do simplify the "drink" situation by stocking two or three kinds of wine and champagne.

8.   For their comfort and ease, do let your guests know what kind of attire fits the occasion.

9.   Do keep hors d'oeuvres light and serve easy predinner nibbles.

10.   If you have extended a dinner invitation more than a week earlier, call and remind your guests of the upcoming date. Things can slip one's mind. (How well I know! I've missed more than one party that way.)

11.   Do set your table — all but the fresh flowers — the night before.

12.   On the day of your party: Relax, read a good book, talk to your flowers, bathe the cat, and enjoy the day.

14.   Be clever, charming, and keep the flow of conversation interesting, rewarding, uplifting and fun. Break up talk-gone-wrong with a sledgehammer if you have to! Redirect the conversation with a joke, a breath of fresh air, or, cause a minor diversion. You can spill water, have your parrot perform cartwheels, or start laughing out loud — any diversion will change the energy in the room, and since it has already taken a dive and gone downhill, it can only get better. Remember, you're in charge, so make it happen.

This is your party!

Chapter Five

Be Prepared

There is a multitude of reasons — and some I haven't heard — for women to break out in a cold sweat, change their name and leave town rather than entertain friends for dinner. They also avoid family gatherings at their homes for no better reason than having the wallpaper changed on that day. And then there are those who have the carpets shampooed, the windows washed, drapery and upholstery cleaned, and the bathrooms sanitized before they will let anyone into the house.

I can relate to some of that. There was a time when my house could pass a white-glove test by the most eagle-eyed flyspeck inspector — including my mother. I don't do that anymore. If I could, I would tear out my wall-to-wall carpeting so that I had a place under which to sweep a bit of dirt — occasionally. If I had the kind of friends and acquaintances who'd come to my home to investigate the level of spic-and-span, glow-and-shine, and sparkle-plenty, I'd never ask them again.

Just remember: soft music, lights turned low, an abundance of candles in corners, and buckets of flowers do more for the ambience than a spotless, flyspeck-free house.

Contrary to all these latter-day child-spoiling experts, it is quite possible to teach children early on to take care of their own things and participate in the upkeep of the family home in such a way that it is fun, and they feel included in "the business of managing a home." I used to invite my two children to participate in my "entertaining" scheme — all they had to do was to stay out of the living and dining rooms that day, and help keep order in the rest of the house. In other words, "Kids, I don't play in your rooms and you don't play in mine." It worked for me, and we had a good time. Today it might qualify as child abuse, who knows?

Since I don't like to spend long hours each week on housework, I do a little bit every day, and I don't seem to notice it. I straighten out the house either before I go to bed at night, or in the morning before the rest of my business day begins. If I get up just thirty minutes before I really "have to" and do a few things around the house, I'm way ahead of the game. It can't compare to clapping your hands to summon your in-house gremlins, or walking on the beach at St. Lucia, but it has its advantages.

I have been accused of being a neatnik about keeping order. That may be so, but I know this: it is much easier to keep order than to make order. Since the living area and kitchen of my house is always presentable, I rarely do more than dust the furniture (flat surfaces only), clean the powder room and kitchen, see that everything is in its place, and arrange the flowers. Total time is less than one hour.

In the evening, when the house is quiet, I turn on my favorite music and go about setting the table. That little girl who would sneak into the big dining room to gawk at the lavishly set dinner table, caress the silky damask cloth and make believe she was the hostess in gossamer silk, has never left. She has her own setting now — vastly different from that other life so long ago, but now she is the hostess. Perhaps I'm still playing house (just forget the gossamer silk!), except I get to do it my way. I always feel that the party is about to start when my table is set. The rest is easy.

The pages of slick magazines offer endless ideas for table decor in articles and advertisements. Lavish settings boggle the mind with their dazzling arrays of precious crystal, costly china and ornate silverware straight from the coffers of Sotheby's or Windsor Castle. It's gorgeous, but it's not reality for most of us.

When you combine that feeling of not having the best, with the over-produced photography of chef-perfect-to-die-for dishes from culinary potboilers, it's no wonder why so many women feel inadequate to entertain in their home. Just remember, you are not competing with the pros, nor do you have to be Martha Perfect. Be your own self, create your own magic, do your own thing — and make it fun.

I don't own priceless treasures that collectors are eyeing with envy. The closest I've come to Gump and Tiffany is flipping through the pages of their beautiful catalogues. Neither do I attempt to outdo the food photographers' glossy imagery, nor do I order expensive centerpieces from the best florist in town. It is a challenge and fun to be creative and to do the best with what you have and can afford. I concentrate my efforts in making my dinner table look different — to make a statement, to set a mood that conveys a sense of humor, a touch of class, and is intended to be a compliment to my guests.

Over the years I have collected some unusual and colorful table settings — some elegant, some whimsical, some downright silly and comical, such as the things I use in my centerpieces for the dinner table. In summer I often scatter my collection of small porcelain and cloisonné birds among a few silver candlesticks and a glass bowl of fresh flowers in the center of the table. Another time, I may let a gang of engaging cloth frogs gather around six clear glass bud vases (some of which are orphan liqueur glasses), each containing a single flower and a fine sprig of green, leaning against a cluster of colorful glass paperweights.

You'd be surprised at the comments these creations evoke, the lightness and chuckles they bring to the table, and how loudly these pieces express the hostess's appreciation of the guests who are cherished in her home.

For fall, I occasionally use several tall, skinny scarecrows I picked up in a card store (inexpensive finds), tiny bales of hay, sprigs of eucalyptus, a few pieces of fresh fruit mixed in with papier mâché copies of fruit. Often I float candles in several balloon-shaped wine glasses for sparkle. It's so simple but it looks great.

Once, two colorful ceramic koi fish and a couple of goofy-charming ceramic mermaid candlesticks followed me home (see illustration). I arrange them around clusters of bud vases with bright flowers to preside over seafood dinners.

Knowing my passion for creating ever-changing table settings, a good friend of mine once presented me with six elegant golden birds the size of sparrows, of unknown materials. Scattered among greens, candles and pieces of glass, they offer their own brand of shimmering magic.

At Christmas time I have used a glass bowl, filled half-full with salt, into which I have sunk three or four votive candles in tiny glass cups. The bowl, placed on a mirror (round, oval or placemat-size), is surrounded with seven-inch glass trees. They are interspersed among old wineglasses filled with water and floating white candles. Small branches of cedar and tiny shimmering stars on a thin gold wire run through the whole arrangement, adding a touch of glitter. The assembly is lovely — all glass, white and gold, and it welcomes table linens of any color.

For a different holiday table setting, I switch to an all white, gold and green centerpiece which consists of fruit and cedar arranged around a trio of tall angels bearing candles. The angels are draped with strands of gold and silver beads. Neither this arrangement nor the one before, is expensive, nor do they demand Martha Perfect's hand-grown, twice-woven, gold-leafed, ever-so-clever manipulations. It takes all of fifteen minutes to put these centerpieces together.

Except for changing the water in the glasses and replacing the candles, the Christmas centerpieces stay fresh and complement the colors in the linens and food I bring to the table.

For a more formal and quite festive table, I position a glass lily which holds just enough water to keep fresh a tiny bouquet of flowers (I prefer a single white tulip) in front of each place setting. I repeat the flower scheme in a low silver bowl in the center of the table, and add several silver candlesticks with tapers to match the color of the flowers.

Sometimes, just for fun, I use place cards. Instead of the cards bearing a guest's name, they carry a short message or observation that fits the individual's personality. It is fun to observe the guests matching the descriptions to themselves and finding their places at the table. This little game takes just a few moments to engineer and adds fresh ammunition to the conversation at the dinner table.

There are times when I arrange garden-variety greenery, fruit, vegetables and candles on a mirror tray, add a few brilliantly colored paperweights from my collection of trivia, and the result is a unique and appealing centerpiece. From your florist you can buy small glass vials with rubbery rims that hold a few drops of water and a flower or two — enough to last an evening, and they can be used again and again. The cost is very small to keep your greenery and sprigs of blossoms fresh and fragrant.

You can use hollowed-out artichokes as a candle base and trim them with greens and a few simple daisies. Fill a big bowl with fruit and vegetables to overflowing and intersperse with fresh flowers in their own water containers.

Small bud vases are inexpensive and lend themselves well to holding a single flower as well as a nosegay, and make for a gracious personal greeting at each place setting. Orefors crystal is magnificent, Waterford creations are majestic, and Bohemian pieces sparkle with their own splendor, but there's nothing wrong with simple, clear glass vases bearing a fresh flower. If we are to avoid being snobbish in our menu choices, as a chef advises, it's just as important to discard the need for upmanship in table accessories. You can do well without the biggest and the best. I do it all the time. It works for me.

Remember what happened to Sleeping Beauty after her mother didn't invite all the nine witches to celebrate her daughter's birth? Mother had only eight golden plates and invited eight guests. The exclusion made the ninth witch mad. I bet you've heard that story! You know what happened.

Every once in a while, I find one of those delightful (I now have four) French "girls," made by some slightly wacky Parisian artist. Their five-inch, shapeless, sack-like bodies are made from a bright fabric and are partially stuffed with birdseed. These silly girls have finely painted porcelain hands, feet, and faces and are topped with unique, wild ceramic headgear. These goofy French sisters, along with a friendly group of small, silk-clad bunnies and other fantasy creatures, often sit among the candlesticks and bud vases in the center of the table. Silly as it may sound, these creatures come to life at the dinner table, are always greeted with great mirth, and are admired and talked about, all of which helps create a carefree, joyous mood.

There is really no end to what you can do in creating interesting, delightful — elegant or whimsical — table settings, as long as you use fresh flowers and candles to enhance your treasures. Think of your decorations as a surprise treat for your guests. Let your imagination roam, and let your table settings become your personal trademark.

I plan the decorations I'm going to use ahead of time, gather up my props, and set a table for eight in as little time as fifteen minutes. If you arrange the flowers the night before, store them in a cool place until the next evening. Keep flowers in the garage, where it is cool in spring and winter. In summer, wrap them loosely in a moist kitchen towel, refrigerate them, and arrange them shortly before your guests are due to arrive. It's one last-minute thing you can do without flirting with disaster. Arranging flowers is not like making a "serve-at-once" soufflé.

Over time, I have accumulated an assortment of placemats, table runners, napery and napkin rings to create color-pleasing combinations that tie it all together. You can assemble memorable and charming table settings that are fun, but in good taste and far removed from the dreaded "kitsch." A well-set table invites very much the same feeling you get from viewing a well-decorated and coordinated window display. You don't want to own just one or two things from the medley on the table in front of you — you want it all because it all goes together, and more than that, it tells a story, it conveys a mood.

❦ ❦ ❦

There are several ways for simplifying the amount of work that can go into a dinner party. For instance, I don't give "theme" parties, such as a Mexican fiesta, a Halloween party, a Roaring Twenties Night, a Hawaiian Luau or an Oktoberfest Polka Hop. I don't like all that crêpe-paper-cardboard-pop-up, theme-oriented cutesy stuff — crinkly streamers, paper flowers, plastic cacti and grass skirts. (I never know what top to wear with a grass skirt. Shucks!)

All that penny-arcade stuff looks better in the high school gym. First of all, such parties can be an awful lot of work and quite costly. Secondly, some people just don't feel comfortable about donning a costume and portraying someone they either want to forget or don't want to be anyway. I am one of those — so is my husband. I know we're not alone; there are lots of people like us.

Just because I may decide to cook an all-German, or Italian, French or Mexican dinner does not mean my guests have to wear a sombrero or lederhosen. I do not turn my living room into the Eiffel Tower — not to mention hanging piñatas. I don't own a dirndl or do after-dinner yodeling, among my other shortcomings. All that is not necessary.

Instead of a theme evening, consider the season, the kind of flowers you may have in the garden or which are readily available, and the kind of people who would enjoy each other at your house. Plan your meal and then go about creating a mood that makes no demands on your guests but celebrates the occasion. You can achieve that just with flowers, candles, and some innovative table settings.

I have to confess my greatest weakness: I would like to own a set of dishes and stemware for every day of the year. I get lost for life in the china section of a department store. My feet stay glued to the sidewalk looking into the windows of a gift store, and for the sake of my health — mental and economic — I don't attend gift shows, and not one of my friends is a rep for Mikasa, Rosenthal or Meissen.

Needless to say, I would have to live in a warehouse, keep a running inventory, and wouldn't have a penny left to feed my family, much less entertain friends. Everything considered, I reluctantly settled for four sets of dishes:

1. China by Sadek, The Nantucket Collection, for a magnificent, colorful gifts-from-the-ocean pattern for seafood dinners.
2. A set of stark white English Coalport china in the raised-rim, it-goes-with-everything Country pattern.
3. Eight each dinner and salad plates of heavy white Portuguese stoneware for casual kitchen dinners are in my collection; and eight oversized antique cut-glass plates I found in a junk store, which I use for serving a first-course salad.
4. For a spring or summer lunch or brunch, indoors or al fresco, I use thick, barely green, scalloped Italian glass plates, along with plain white linens and

pinkish-red, floppy, silk flower napkin rings. The plates are gorgeous — but then you know all about those gorgeous, stunning, appealing Italians!

That's all. Any more dishes and I would have to add on to the house, or move into a shopping mall.

(I forgot to mention eight gold-lacquered chargers, and a few interesting odds and ends. You won't tell anyone, please.)

I use different kinds of stemware for different effects: Heavy crystal goblets for a more formal table; sturdy pale green Mexican stems for the sake of color and shape and variety, and slim, tall (clear and colored) glass goblets for their fragile, graceful go-with-everything look.

The stark white dishes, combined with clear stemware, provide me with unlimited opportunities to bring a variety of colors, patterns and textures to the table. Even though the dishes I use are always the same, flowers, placemats, linens, napery, napkin rings, and my "guess-who's-coming-to-dinner" accessories are a surprise that conjure up a totally different feeling and mood every time.

None of the things I own are priceless treasures, exquisite heirlooms or registered museum pieces. Everything I possess is replaceable. I don't mourn broken glass or sob over shards of porcelain. My old Chinese teacher told me years ago: "The loss of anything that money can buy is not worth crying over." You know, he was right.

With an eye out for savings and with a firm rein on my unbridled passion for hoarding, I buy candles when the price is right and always have a good supply on hand. I buy them in several colors and shapes to fit my assortment of votive holders and candlesticks and the rest of the table decor.

In order to avoid a last-minute switch of table linens or placemats, I play Nancy Neatnik and keep my linens freshly laundered, ironed and ready for the next occasion.

One bit of advice: keep your centerpieces for the dinner table at a reasonable height, so that the flow of conversation across the table doesn't resemble something between a game of hide-and-seek and peek-a-boo. When I look at some of the table settings in home decor magazines and see tall candelabra with extra-long tapers among the reach-for-the-ceiling flower and fruit arrangements in containers that resemble a Swiss Alpenhorn, I can only surmise that the display was arranged by the Jolly Green Giant. It would be impossible to carry on a conversation, much less see the person to whom you address your comments across such a barricade.

If you like music in your home, remember to keep the volume at "background low" only. It is hard to converse over blaring trumpets or thumping drums. Tastes in music differ, and you may wish to select some light classical melodies (nothing bombastic, please) or other pleasant sounds for easy background music. Everything you do dictates the mood of the evening. So make it pleasant for your friends as well as for yourself.

To repeat a line I used before, entertaining is not an act of competition, nor is it for impressing the neighbors. It is simply a gracious gesture to share a meal in a setting that spawns conviviality, coddles the guests, and makes them feel important and cherished.

And always remember: Your guests are the stars of your production, but without any doubt, you are the director, in charge of the script (conversation), lighting, stage setting, props and music.

Above all, keep it simple. Elegance is born of simplicity — simply elegant!

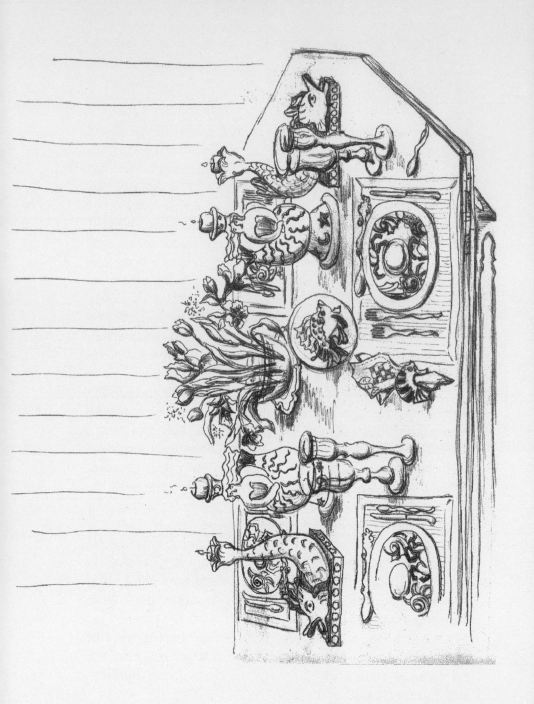

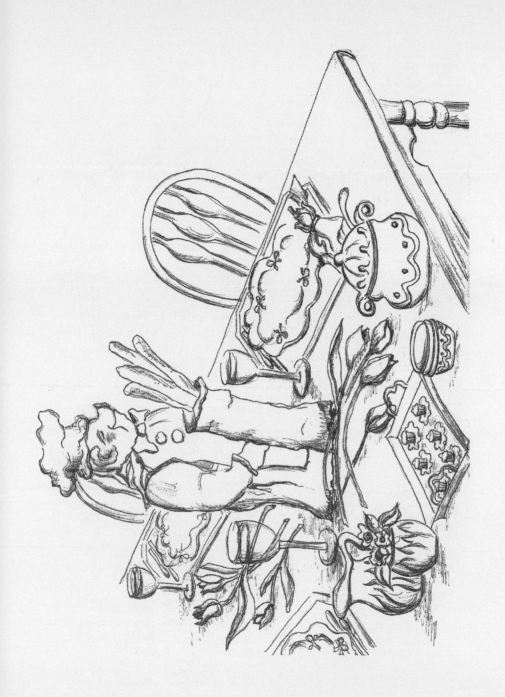

Chapter Six

Your Pantry – Your Cupboard – Your Freezer – Your Refrigerator

Time Spent is Time Saved

There is nothing more frustrating than to be all set to start cooking, round up the ingredients, and come up empty-handed with something you need. Whether you live in the country, five miles away from the nearest store, or next door to your best-friend-neighbor, running out to buy or borrow at the last moment is a nuisance and a time waster. By the time you get back from the errand, you could well be out of the mood. The last time I borrowed something from my darling neighbor was a disaster. I stayed for two hours, caught up on the latest, had three glasses of wine, came home and went to bed with a headache. Of course, I didn't get anything done in my kitchen, nor anywhere else.

Another thing I won't do is to send my husband to the store. The few times I tried, he came back with the strangest things that ranged from wine-soaked butterflied anchovy fillets, garlic-stuffed capers, to Limburger croissants. I fully believe that some things are on the shelves just because men will buy them, not that they ever eat them!

Fortunately, as I mentioned before, I am a closet hoarder. There are still vestiges of my refugee days hovering in my soul, and the urge to be prepared, to be ready for all kinds of what-ifs needs to be stilled. Therefore, my cupboard is rarely empty, the freezer and refrigerator are well-stocked, and my pantry is always full. I have the annoying habit of buying two or more of everything from staples, canned goods, condiments to candles, to special treats and cheeses. I hold back on overloading on spices only because they do lose their potency and flavor when they get old.

I stockpile ingredients so that I can produce a feast on short notice. I also precook and freeze (see recipe section) main courses ready to come to the table at the drop of a hat. There are always two kinds of dessert in my freezer, along with several loaves of ready-to-bake garlic bread, and (purchased) bite-size mini-quiches for nibbles. Taking all my hoarding into consideration, my husband insists that I could keep our neighborhood fed for one month, and I could easily qualify for being a one-stop rural shopping experience.

I'm really not as bad about hoarding as some people I know, who can't even lay claim to having been a refugee. I remember Nancy, a former neighbor and dear friend of mine. She made a career of stocking up such quantities of food and supplies that would have made the quartermaster of an invading army proud. Her husband insisted that the new shopping center a mile away could never have made it without his wife's faithful daily patronage.

Nancy called me one day, asking me if I needed any butter, cottage cheese, eggs or sour cream. In other words, would I like to go shopping at her house? As it turned out, she cleaned out her two huge refrigerators, and to her amazement came up with twelve pounds of butter, nine dozen (aged) eggs, eight large containers of cottage cheese and six pints of sour cream — the latter turning off-white and growing beards. It then dawned on me why her husband wouldn't let her buy a freezer!

I'm not that bad — close though I may be — but I have a freezer!

The following items are always on my shelves. If you have limited storage space, keep on hand at least one or two of each item you use regularly.

Stocking the Pantry

Apart from the normal staples like flour, sugar, cornstarch, baking soda, etc., these are the things I always keep on hand:

- Raisins and currants
- Almond paste
- Baking chocolate
- Crystallized ginger
- Chocolate mousse (prepared in powder form)
- Custard (prepared in powder form)
- Instant espresso coffee
- Dried mushrooms (a variety)
- Dried onion soup
- *Knorr* sauce mixes: Hollandaise, Bearnaise
- *Knorr* vegetable soup
- Vanilla wafers
- Graham cracker crumbs
- Chocolate wafers
- A complete set of spices — one of everything!

- Raspberry syrup
- *Oetker* glaze (clear)

Canned Goods Hoard

I keep several cans of the following:
- Cut Italian stewed tomatoes
- Stewed regular tomatoes
- Tomato paste
- Tomato purée
- Beef broth
- Chicken broth
- Vegetable broth
- Consommé
- Mushrooms
- Clam juice
- Olives (whole and chopped)
- *Ortega* green peppers
- Bamboo shoots
- *V-8* juice
- Water chestnuts
- Corn
- Asparagus
- Pickled beets
- Spiced apple slices (garnish)
- Canned pears
- Dark cherries
- Jams and jalapeño jelly

Add your "must-haves" to this list!

Stocking the Refrigerator

First, your regular things, plus condiments. Also:
- One-half pint whipping cream
- One pint half and half
- Eight-ounce wheel of brie
- One chunk parmesan cheese
- Three eight-ounce packages cream cheese
- Puff pastry
- Phyllo

Stocking the Freezer

- Two pounds butter
- Tiny green peas
- One pound crabmeat
- Two pounds lean ground beef
- Two pounds large shrimp
- Two pounds lean beef stew
- Six chicken breasts
- One pound chicken livers
- One package gnocchi
- One pound linguine
- One pound vegetarian ravioli
- One pound angel hair pasta
- One cheesecake
- One nut torte
- Two loaves garlic bread, ready for the oven
- One to two pounds Italian sausage (chicken)
- Two complete dinners: One Lasagna Bolognese and one Ham and Noodle Casserole
- Anything else precooked and ready for "just in case"

Stocking Up on "Stuff"

Sauces:
- Tabasco
- Worcestershire
- Piccata
- Gourmet sauce
- Maggi
- Teriyaki glaze/sauce
- Barbecue sauce
- Chili sauce
- Savory sauce
- Vinegars
- Walnut oil
- Anchovy paste

Mustards:
- Sweet and tart
- Stone ground

Liquors (for cooking purposes only):
- Apple brandy
- Pernod
- Triple sec
- Port
- Sherry
- Marsala
- Vermouth
- Red wine
- Dry white wine.

This may seem like a lot of booze, but believe me (unless you do a little nipping here and there, which is okay by me), it will last a long time.

Favorite Kitchen Stuff

As much as is humanly possible, I stay out of kitchen stores. In my saner moments, with my eyes shut tightly, I toss Mr. Soo Nami's, the Pottery Shed's and Chef Delight's fine catalogs out of my sight. I'm not really that gadget-happy, but I'm vulnerable. I've been known to walk into cook shops and buy a thing or two, and I have ordered "stuff" from catalogs in sleepwalker fashion.

Most of the time, I tell myself I don't need a $180 mandolin or balalaika for slicing cucumbers all of six times a year. Unlike Martha Perfect, I don't have a pasta or a bread machine. I don't want to be responsible for the decline of the bread and pasta industries. But I do have an automatic garlic peeler that works garlic magic.

If you consider updating your outdated kitchen gadgetry, here are some special things you might want to acquire. If you do, buy the best; they'll outlive anybody, even Julia-Julia. The list that follows consists of my must-have kitchen tools but doesn't mention most standard gadgets we all have.

Pots and Pans

One eight-quart stock pot with inset for spaghetti cooking
    *(Calphalon)**
One seventeen-inch double-handled skillet *(Calphalon)**
One double boiler, clear glass *(Pyrex)**
One four-piece set of *Corning Ware** or other saucepans
    *Footnote: I am not endorsing brands (I'm not getting paid for it, darn it). It just so happens that I have used a lot of different pots and pans over the years until I settled for the ones that work best for me.

Electrical Cooking Gadgets

One *Cuisinart** — top of the line — you won't regret it
One hand-held electric mixer
One hand-held electric blender (great for straightening out
    lumpy gravy and other cooking hazards)
One large electric skillet with a tall lid
Electric handy chopper *(Black and Decker*)*

Just Gadgets

Garlic peeler (no kidding!)
Instant-read meat thermometer
Pear corer
Garlic press
Small wood cutting board
Lemon/lime/orange zester
Flat-bottomed wire whisk
One four-sided, six-inch-tall shredder-grater
Oven mitts
Eight to twelve (custard-size) glass bowls (for setting out
    measured ingredients)
Rubber scrapers, wooden spoons, kitchen shears, pliers,
    tongs, non-electric juicer, sieves, colanders, steam
    basket, and anything else that makes you feel good
One set of excellent knives, from small paring to large "can-
    handle-that-turkey-or-roast carving knife
One Chinese cleaver
One hand-held rolling mincer — the undisputed star in my
    kitchen
One decorative six-quart tureen with ladle (gorgeous!)

One three-piece set of springform pans
One each oval, round and oblong white *Corning Ware**
 baking dishes in various sizes, including a large, deep
 one to hold a lasagna
One complete set of *Pyrex** bakeware
Muffin tins, cookie sheets — but you already have those if
 you know what's good for you.

❦ ❦ ❦

    I'd better stop now. You must have caught the drift,
and you most probably have been cooking for a while. If
you haven't, you just may want to run right out and buy all
that stuff. And if you still don't like to cook, you may want
to get your money back and buy a "round-the-world" ticket
on the next ship out. As fate has it, there is a chef on board,
and room service is on the menu.

Chapter Seven

That's Entertainment

*Let me entertain you and we'll all have a
really good time.*
– Gypsy Rose Lee

Not long ago, an article in *W* magazine — the chi-chi
edition of *Women's Wear Daily* — often referred to
as the *International Jetters and Wannabe Funnies*
— reported on the latest, absolutely must-do for moneyed
newcomers to the *haute monde* scene who are anxious to
climb the precarious ladder to the lofty heights of social
acceptance. The article explained all about perfecting
hostessing skills for those who have missed out at an earlier
stage, or were born on the wrong side of the dinner table. It
happens, you know! Those with questionable social skills
can enroll in a week-long finishing course for adults
conducted in the remote Scottish Highlands. There, a
society-savvy countess with a long name has started *Savoir*

Faire, Savoir Vivre (How to Do and How to Live). The short course promises graduates something akin to a degree in entertaining, and the coveted Golden Skillet Award.

For a hefty five-figure fee (social acceptance doesn't come cheap) students learn to "manage a household staff, create atmosphere, arrange flowers, and hostess." (I do so worry about managing my household staff — don't you?)

The countess is dedicated to imparting her deepest secrets to her wealthy but still-a-bit-rough-around-the-social-edges students of *nouveau riche* status by offering classroom lectures on social graces, including:

- How to conduct a dinner conversation.
- How to behave in the inner circles of Balmoral, Le Cirque, Mercedes Chantilly's drawing room, and other social fortresses.
- How to plan seating arrangements.
- How to properly introduce people.
- How to write a letter of condolence. (Don't ever forget those who've passed on; you never know when you may meet them again — especially at those stately, tradition-riddled men's clubs.)
- Flower arranging. (I guess it helps having a household staff, which would leave time for flower arranging.)

On the other side of the coin, she admonishes her students to "be a gracious guest ... to be attractive, entertaining and amusing."

That's class! Now you know where you can buy it.

Here's a little more about "class" on the down-to-earth plane, and it concerns being a great guest:

Although it is not a fast rule, it is common practice for some people, and I heartily agree, not to arrive at someone's house — including a Scottish castle — empty-handed.

Bring something little, not a gift of grandeur, but rather an expression of thanks, a thoughtful gesture. A bunch of flowers, a single rose, a gift book, a poem, a potted pansy, a loaf of bread, a bottle of wine, a jar of....

A day or so after the party, please send a thank-you note, or call your hostess to let her know how much you enjoyed the evening, and how much you appreciated her efforts. Don't for a moment think that expressing your gratitude at parting is enough. It is not! Take time, your time, to convey to your host or hostess what the event has meant to you. It is truly the gracious thing to do. Just think how you would like your guests to respond, and you'll do the right thing. But you already knew that, didn't you?

Another sure way to qualify for the Golden Gracious Guest Award is to respond promptly to the RSVP on invitations. Should there be a change in your life as late as a day before the party, let your hostess know. She might be paying a premium per-person fee to a caterer and will appreciate to be advised of the change in attendance. (If you're a good hostess, you already are a good guest.)

Those of us who simply can't make it to the remote Scottish Highlands to attend the chic and socially acceptable countess's next finishing course, will just have to activate Plan B.

Plan B is simple — void of social acrobatics, up-the-ladder gymnastics or personal manipulations. Entertaining costs nothing more than a little time, effort and thoughtfulness. Plan B takes us back to basics. It serves as a reminder that getting together with friends and acquaintances in your home, preparing a meal, exchanging ideals and ideas, creating an enjoyable atmosphere, is a gift to your guests as well as a benefit to yourself. It is a grand way people have of celebrating each other. That's entertainment!

For the guests to be "entertained" requires the hostess to stay out of the kitchen and spend time with them — to make them feel welcome, comfortable and pampered. Trips to the stove are of course necessary to move dinner along. For that reason I recommend you sit at the edge of the circle, close to the kitchen, so that your slipping away is less noticeable. Make it a point to stay with your guests until a smooth flow of conversation has been established, and people are indeed comfortable with each other. If you have a co-host — husband, friend or partner, see to it that one of you remains with your guests. It can be awkward when both host and hostess leave their friends on their own by disappearing into the kitchen to get dinner going, especially if they are first-time guests.

If good conversation is slow to emerge, take over and steer it in a more stimulating direction. That's why four to six guests is the ideal number for staying on top of the subject matter that fuels the flow of the conversation.

This is as good a place as any to talk about a most unique friend of mine, her equally unique hotel, and her splendid way of running things in a way that made Goody Cable and her establishments a legend in her time. My friend not only is a superb people collector, but she possesses an insatiable curiosity about them and everything else that makes the world go around — the very qualities which are the sign of an irresistible hostess.

Several years ago, Goody was looking for a site on the Oregon coast she could turn into the kind of hotel only she could envision. She wanted a place where people could think, exchange ideas and experience themselves surrounded by the splendor of the Pacific Northwest.

She found it. The building was a vacant, rundown structure with a bad memory when Goody came across the derelict structure ten years ago, and rescued the venerable walls from impending doom and destruction. Restored to a comfortably old-fashioned place of solitude, good books and quiet fame, *Sylvia Beach Hotel* at Newport, Oregon, now attracts a string of interesting and famous people who come from thousands of miles and book their next stay a year and more in advance.

The guest rooms are named after well-known authors and are furnished in the style of their era, enhanced by memorabilia. There are no radios, television sets or telephones in any of the rooms. The third-floor library, with its well-stocked shelves, faces the Pacific Ocean and provides all the stimuli, entertainment and dream time the hotel guests seek.

Dinner is served family-style in a comfortable dining room at round tables for eight — the perfect number for conversation. At the end of a fine meal, Sylvia Beach Hotel tradition takes over. A game of *Two Truths and One Lie* is played at each table. Tradition is rarely wrong, because this particular game is tailor-made for people to get well-acquainted, to discover something special about each other, and unite them in a common interest. It goes something like this:

One person starts by telling two truths and one lie about herself or himself, and the seven dinner partners at the table have to guess which statement is the lie. For example:

1. When I was young, I worked in the Colorado mines and nearly froze to death.
2. My father built the plane that Lindbergh flew across the Atlantic.
3. I lunched at the White House.

Each guest may direct one question to the storyteller, make his decision, and render his verdict as to which is the lie.

This may be a game, but it does get the dinner guests involved in only one topic of discussion at their table, one conversation. There is no room for aside chatting, and that simple act alone unifies eight people concentrating on one subject, giving their full attention to each individual. By the end of the evening, people have discovered fascinating and interesting facts about each other, continue to explore and expand ideas, and more often than not make friends for life. It is not unusual for people to part with a fervent "same-time-same-place-next-year" promise — and keep it.

Goody accomplished what she set out to do: create a mood, an atmosphere for people to embrace and make their own. The hotel, its furnishings and the fine food are simply props. It is the spirit of the house — and there is such a thing — that draws and embraces visitors in a state of irresistible grace and charm, which is exactly what a hostess wants to achieve in her home.

When you set the scene and promote brisk conversation, there's little room for small talk and directionless chatter. When your guests finally break up, they may leave your home with a faint memory of a good meal — but more than anything, they will take along the lasting gift of having experienced a stimulating evening in a never-to-be-forgotten setting. That's entertainment!

When you are thinking of inviting four or six or so people for dinner — stop! — ponder their interests, consider their temperaments and their abilities to contribute to a lively gathering. You are looking for a fit, some common ground, a blending of personalities that enhance and complement each other. By no means do I want to imply that people always have to think alike or that their professional backgrounds should match. If you invite people who are in the same "business" — all doctors, all lawyers, all scientists, politicians, tinkers, tailors or Indian chiefs — just imagine what most of the conversation would be like. The "pros" will mostly talk about their business.

When that happens, the other half of your guests will choose a subject of their interests, and all of a sudden you get exactly what you didn't want — several conversations going on at the same time as everyone rattles on about her or his interests. Remember that awful incident at the Tower of Babel? Well, don't let that scene play out in your living room or at the dinner table.

Let it go for a little while, wait for an opening — or create a clever diversion yourself — then change the subject quickly, which brings everyone together. If this sounds complicated and overly involved — it really isn't. It's quite simple to change the conversation and, by so doing, change the course of the evening.

You can do it when you put your mind to it. Entertaining takes some planning, direction and thought, and it also takes the courage of your convictions to establish "definite house rules." It demands an ample display of honesty wrapped in a satiny mantle of diplomacy in order to avoid unnecessary and awkward situations. It's self-protection — more like karate for the soul.

Remember, you're the hostess, the director of the play, and there are equal rights for hostesses.

Here are some suggestions for eliminating dreaded moments:

1. Embarrassing dinner menus: Always ask a first-time guest about food dislikes or dietary restrictions.

I had to experience an incident at my dinner table before I caught on to that simple trick. I prepared a meal of delicious Indian shrimp curry, only to discover to my dismay that two of my four first-time guests were highly allergic to shellfish. Somebody else hated curry with a passion. Great!

Picking out the shrimp and just serving the broth with its ample amount of vegetables didn't work either because the shrimp had left enough of their characteristics to cause a serious allergic reaction. Next to settling for a bologna or peanut butter and jelly sandwich, my gracious guests ended up with hot French bread, plain rice and a salad — and a double serving of Black Forest Trifle as a reward.

I was mortified, but I learned my lesson.

2. The same thought for personal preferences applies to the serving of alcohol.

I gave up stocking an open bar years ago. Instead, I settled for offering a dry white wine (a Chardonnay and a dry Riesling) a good red wine (a light-hearted Merlot and a richer Cabernet Sauvignon or Pinot Noir), and Cook's, my favorite champagne. Offering only wine has become a most accepted custom, especially on the West Coast; however, if you have a well-stocked bar, use your best judgment for what to serve your guests. If a guest turns down your offer of a glass of wine in preference for a non-alcoholic drink, don't push for an explanation. Your friend may be a recovering alcoholic, or doesn't drink on Arbor Day — whatever. That is not your business.

3. Advise your guests what kind of attire is appropriate for the occasion.

There exists such an overwhelming trend for throwing on "casual" garments today and a nagging resistance to "getting dressed" that you have to let your guests know what you expect of them. An elegant friend of mine, a grand host himself and former diplomat, mourned the passing of certain ways when he stated: "Most people rarely wear real clothes anymore. They just toss on an odd assortment of rather unattractive outer coverings."

I believe that when I've spent time and money in preparation for a festive evening, I would like my guests to honor that gesture by dressing for the occasion. So, if you don't want your guest to arrive in sweats and tennies, let them know what you expect of them.

You can be quite tactful, yet succinct, in your suggestions. Let them know what you are wearing. Simply tell first-time guests:

"In case you wonder what to wear, let me tell you that my husband was born in grey flannels and a turtleneck — he wears a tie only under duress, and I usually find a long skirt or a pair of silk pants with a fun top." More often than not, this serves as a guideline for "when-in-doubt" persons.

There are a hundred ways to discourage someone from wearing jeans and worn-out sneakers. I may tell first-time guests to "wear something you wouldn't wear on a three-mile hike, the Boston Marathon, or to a barn-raising event. Put something on that is comfortable but makes you feel pampered and even a bit festive. After all, you are going out for dinner."

Perhaps this request for dressing up a bit sounds old-fashioned, opinionated, or even dictatorial in a time where casual is in, where comfort is everything, and where grunge has been transplanted from the back alleys to the front room. I don't care if the sweatshirt costs $150 and the embroidered polo player on the pocket jumps on the table and swings his mallet at a green pea — it's still a sweatshirt.

When I threw this subject out for discussion at a luncheon gathering not long ago, one young career woman quipped smartly, "I tell my guests not to wear anything they wouldn't dare put on to visit the Queen of England. I'm no different." Well, I guess, all isn't lost yet!

I believe fully that this whole issue has to do with respect, good taste and a set of simple social values that some people may consider old-fashioned, outdated and too frumpy for the cyberspace age. I want to know, what's wrong with dressing well? When I am invited to someone's house, I honor my host's world. It may not be what I would do or like, or even feel comfortable with — but then it is not my world.

On a recent plane ride on a hot summer day in a crowded aircraft without a deep breath to spare, I got stuck sitting next to a man wearing a food-stained, off-white undershirt with elongated underarm cuts that disappeared into his dangerously small running shorts. He was dressed perfectly for joining a hunting party in the Kalahari Desert without the benefit of a deodorant. In other words, his *Ban* had long rolled off. Obviously, this man didn't give a hoot about how his attire affected a whole planeload of people, or, as my daughter charitably put it, "he probably didn't have a mother." Unfortunately, there are more like him, and they don't limit their tacky, unkempt attire to airplanes.

What about those youngsters whose turned-around baseball caps are grafted to their heads, and whose clothes were rescued from the last closet in Haight-Ashbury — all of which their parents ignore, even in the stately confines of the lovely dining rooms of fine restaurants. Oh, well, I'd better get off my soapbox, and give it back to Mush Bimbo.

My grumpiness may appear unrelated to this book, but I am offended by people who are rude, display contempt for graciousness and manners, and whose impolite arrogance in sloppy dress and behavior indicates the absence of taste and social discipline. Believe me, graciousness has everything to do with entertaining and with personal custom. (But then, you know what I mean.)

I remember an episode from years ago. We often entertained business associates and friends who were our suppliers. A national manufacturer's habit of transferring department heads and replacing them with newcomers to our area was a recurring event. We always welcomed the new couple with a dinner party and included a few of their new local colleagues.

One such set of newcomers from the East Coast eagerly accepted my Saturday night dinner invitation. I must have forgotten to tell them what to wear. When I answered the door that evening, there stood before me a handsome couple about my age, slightly damp and disheveled, clad in rumpled jogging suits and stained sneakers, still panting from the exertion of running. wiping their brows with soggy Kleenex.

"Hi! We discovered that we live only ten blocks away from you," the husband informed me jubilantly, "so we decided to get in some exercise before dinner, and jog on over." His partner in crime, a petite perspiring brunette, finished his sentence, bubbling over breathlessly with her own cleverness at such a feat.

Isn't that precious?

After a quick glance at my long skirt and silk shirt, the young woman let go with another gush of words in a more mournful tone of voice: "Oh, dear," she groaned, "we didn't know we were supposed to 'dress'."

Where did the little darling think she was going? To a neighborhood track meet?

My reply may have surprised them a bit when I suggested — ever so sweetly, of course — "How convenient you live only ten blocks away. Why don't you jog on back home, take a quick shower and get dressed. Come back, and do use the car this time. I'll hold dinner. Hurry back, now — you hear?"

One hour later the doorbell rang. Two well-dressed, scrubbed-pink people, pushing a handful of yellow roses at me as a peace offering, greeted me diplomatically, a big grin spreading over their glowing faces, "So nice of you to invite us. I hope we haven't kept you waiting."

Later on, Susan, the young wife, confessed gratefully that it was the best lesson they ever learned in the social graces department: how to be a good guest, and how to be a hostess with convictions. We became good friends.

The following issues can be touchy ones and require that "iron-fist-in-velvet-glove" approach. I have to admit that I had to gather up all my courage in dealing honestly with these situations:

You have invited two or three couples for dinner. They know you have planned one of your "intimate little dinners" for six or eight, as the case may be. It is about two hours or so before your guests are to arrive. The telephone rings. Here it comes, preceded by a brief but jubilant declaration of how much they are looking forward to coming to dinner. They can hardly contain their excitement as they gush one of the following "little change of plans:"

A. My mother and father-in-law (my cousin's roommate, Aunt Millie from Philly) are in town for a few days. I'd l-o-v-e for you to meet them, and I'd l-o-v-e to bring them to dinner. That's all right, isn't it?"

(Great! We're now playing Guess Who's Coming to Dinner.)

B. "We have a marvelous surprise for you! We have a darling, three-month-old St. Bernard puppy, and we can't leave her alone yet. Would you mind if we brought Erika along? You'll just l-o-v-e her, and you won't have to worry about feeding her. We'll bring her food."

Does that mean she won't eat the carpet and the furniture? Well, have you ever seen a three-month-old St. Bernard puppy? Let me assure you, the word "puppy" hardly applies.

C. "Our babysitter can't come tonight; her pet goat ate her roller blades. We can't get another sitter. We have to bring the children (just three little darlings aged three to nine). They just l-o-v-e you, and I know you're crazy about them!"

Thanks for sharing! They can have a picnic on the den floor!

D. "We've just discovered that we've had this invitation to attend an open house for the longest time. We've got to make an appearance! I hope you won't mind if we run a couple of hours late."

Shucks! (Let's see, that delays the dinner hour to about ten o'clock.)

E. "Hello, dear one! We're so-o-o-o looking forward to seeing you tonight. (I already know what's coming — don't you?) I hope you won't mind if we watch the Hoopers play the Ringers during dinner tonight. You know our passion for basketball; we're such fans of the Hoopers."

Don't they know our television set is in the upstairs bedroom, bricked-in on the wall behind an eight-foot armoire the Green Bay Packers couldn't budge?

I am always tempted to reply to such requests in the same manner in which Lucy *(I Love Lucy)* might have responded to her best friend, Ethel:

Do call me when:

... your out-of-town guests have left.

... your dog Erika is back in Switzerland working an avalanche.

... your sitter has a new set of roller blades and has gotten rid of her pet goat.

... you're not invited somewhere else and you'll be two hours late to my dinner party.

... your favorite team is on Social Security and they own a barbershop.

... your thoughtfulness has vastly improved.

All smart remarks aside, it took me quite some time to be courageous and honest, stick by my guns, and — as graciously as possible — say:

"Golly-gee-whiz, I'm so sorry, but that just won't work this time ... wish it would ... I'll wish you were here ... I'm terribly sorry, golly-gee-whiz, hate to miss meeting-seeing so-and-so and-so-and-so ... may I give you a rain check, please. Let's try for another time when it's more convenient for *you,* darlings."

If that person is offended by your response, then this individual doesn't know any better and you haven't lost a thoughtful friend — you just outgrew a problem. We all outgrow some people in the course of living. Some of us get left behind, and some we leave behind as we grow and our intellectual, emotional and spiritual requirements take on a different slant. And that's quite all right. Can you imagine yourself still talking junior-high stuff, discussing senior-high events, and debating college freshman opinions?

UGH! Take out my mind and dust it off!

That brings me to the matter of meeting new people and inviting them to my home. I have discovered a long time ago that if I want the world in my living room, I can't wait for the world to knock on my front door. I have to go out, find it, invite it in, and make it my own. I rarely wait around to be discovered and usually take the first step to what often turn out to become lasting friendships. Those who call me a people collector may just have a point. "The world is full of wonderful people, and I know them all," seems to be my motto. (The turkeys don't count.)

I remember a very distinguished, brilliant, but crusty, international lecturer and his equally awesome wife whom I had the good fortune to meet at someone's home, and a short time later invited to dinner. We had discovered our similar backgrounds and interests (not in regards to science or being in the genius category), and I was looking forward to an evening peppered with the professor's own brand of sizzling comments, fascinating ideas and sparkling conversation.

He responded to my invitation with delight, but crisply added the conditions under which he would accept: "I come at six, I eat at seven, and I don't drink red wine." Nothing pompous about that one!

I gathered all my courage, loaded my voice with warmth, a handful of chuckles and all the "charm" I could muster and replied, "Great, darling. But you'll have to do that at your house. At my house you come at seven, you eat at eight, and we won't fuss about the wine. We can't wait to see you."

I must have managed to put enough of something in my voice, because after just the briefest silence, he roared a well-modulated, "Damn you; we'll see you at seven!" and hung up. (Maybe he was just hungry?)

He arrived with his lovely wife at seven o'clock sharp, bearing a heavenly bunch of flowers, trying to look a bit put-upon and suffering. His phony air of injured grandeur didn't last long, as he quickly got caught up in conversation with the other guests. Perfectly content, he sipped — not so daintily — a glass of sparkling white wine. Easy! We became very good friends, and he never played his accustomed role of the hard-to-get guest again.

The next thing that continually comes up upon inviting people to dinner is the thoughtful question: "What may I bring?" in reference to food or drink. I simply thank my caller profusely for the lovely gesture but decline the offer. "Nothing, thank you; it's all done. Just bring yourself (… or bring Dave, or John or what's-his-name.) Don't worry about food; come and enjoy." You may have a different idea about this matter — that's okay too. I guess it goes back to managing the evening your way, and serving the kind of food you had planned, prepared, and of which there is plenty!

Let your guests know in a gracious way if you don't want help with clearing the table or cleaning up in the kitchen. I want my friends to relax and enjoy the evening. I don't want to interrupt the flow of conversation by having one or two jump up, gather a few dishes, and bring them into the kitchen. I tell my friends: "You don't work in my house, I don't work in yours."

To add to your guests' comfort, wait to clear a course until everybody has finished. The slowpoke eater will be grateful for your gracious gesture. Don't you just love it when you're dining out, have taken three bites, rested your fork for a second, and some server appears at your elbow, and with the words "Are you finished?" attempts to whisk away your full dinner plate? I have decided the place is short of dishes, or that they sell the same portion twice with a few minor adjustments to it. (Just watch out for that "server" with a puncture wound in the back of his hand; he tried to take my *plate du jour* away from me.)

Here I go again — being the controller. But I have developed a fairly quick and quiet way of whisking dishes off of the table, slipping them into the kitchen, stacking them in the dishwasher and returning with the dessert. When we retire to the living room after dinner, I leave the rest of plates and glasses on the table.

Oh, well, it will all be there for me long after my guests have departed. Most of the time, my husband clears the table after he's tucked our guests into their cars, and while I finish up and put things away, I keep running the evening back in my mind, and before I know it my work is done. Who wants to wake up to a dirty kitchen? I'd never get up! It takes me no more than twenty minutes to clean up and remove all traces of having prepared and served dinner for eight — except for those leftovers, of course. They come in handy the next day, and the flowers will stay fresh for days, if you keep them in a cool place overnight.

Believe me, superwoman I'm not. But I'm doing what I'm doing because I really enjoy myself. You know what "they" say: "Time flies when you're having a good time." And, as I said before, my recreation is cooking and my passion is people. Entertaining is just like a good novel: a good novel is not about events, it is about people.

Remember: A dinner party is not about food, it is about people!

Chapter Eight

Give It a Try — You'll Like It!

*Cooking is a gracious, warm and nurturing
kind of thing to offer people.
For others, like me, cooking is like therapy. It
is totally relaxing, absorbing and a great outlet
for stored-up energy. It's creative; it's giving.*
– author unknown

Women use more excuses for not wanting to cook than
there are seeds in a fifty-pound watermelon. And, like a
seed, the excuses take root and grow into more excuses or
watermelons — depending on what you're planting. The
answer to the dilemma lies in learning to master a few
simple steps:
1. Don't panic!
2. Do a little research (nothing too deep) to find out
   what you dislike most about entertaining.
3. Recognize the priorities of entertaining.

4. Bring together the people who will make the evening for you. (Don't invite a bore to dinner — send him one!)

5. Change your attitude about cooking.

6. Practice preparing several menu choices so that you know them by heart. Remember: No matter what you want to learn, you will have to study and you will have to practice.

7. Organize your kitchen for easy access to utensils and ingredients. Alphabetize your collection of herbs and spices, arrange pantry and refrigerator, categorizing your supplies, and you will be able to find what you want with your eyes closed.

One caution: Before you administer that "dash" of a spice directly to the dish under preparation, check the inner cover of the spice jar to be sure it's there and, furthermore, fits snugly over the opening of the container. Don't think it hasn't happened. I've done it more than once! I've managed to dump full containers of cayenne pepper, paprika, cinnamon and curry powder into the pot with its wonderful contents just because the clear plastic inner lid of the jar was missing or loose. That kind of seasoning causes heartburn for the septic tank.

There is absolutely nothing you can do about it. It won't come off — it's a dump! And, unless you have an emergency meal in the freezer, you may have to serve cereal or take the gang out to dinner.

Arrange your pantry by categories of food, so that when you need a can of chicken broth, it will be in your "soup section." Otherwise you have to plow through the rest of your canned goods to locate it. Keep your pantry like the shelves of a grocery store — and, just like your favorite store, everything will be at your fingertips.

Keep your freezer contents in a certain order that works for you. I separate meat and poultry from breads, vegetables and pre-cooked dinners. I label and date everything, including leftovers. I've learned to be orderly from my mistakes. Years ago, I used to toss things into the freezer in a manner that could be compared to scattering wild flower seeds in the back pasture. Eons later, with the help of an Antarctic-trained archeological team, I retrieved unrecognizable lumps of foods of ice-age characteristics — not fit for a polar bear.

Lack of organization is expensive. It produces waste. Invest the time to make and keep order, and you will save time later on.

8.   Be prepared for unexpected guests. Keep a well-stocked larder and, if possible, stash a pre-cooked dinner or two in your freezer.

9.   Do not set yourself up to fail — no five-star, thirty-five-step gourmet-magazine acrobatics.

10.   Plan the evening for your enjoyment, as well as for your guests.'

11.   Keep it simple.

I know, you can always find a good caterer or invest your money in a take-out gourmet deli. However, the price you pay for fine take-out-gourmet deli fixings or in-house catering services may make you feel you just bought the store — or the catering business, for that matter. Just remember, you still want to create the mood, the house, the flowers, the candles, the table, the people — The Mood. It's more important than the food.

Cooking is just like any other craft you wish to tackle and eventually master. It takes an adjusted frame of mind, a banishing of fear of failure, some practice and — as Julia Child recommends — "a what-the-hell attitude."

One Manhattan attorney compared cooking to his work: "Cooking and law are quite similar. With both, there is the challenge of problem solving, logic and reasoning." He must be a different lawyer, I bet. He's not all jury, judge and jail, retainers and libel. Anybody who loves to cook can't be all attorney.

To me, cooking is fun — creative and satisfying. There, I've said it again! I often escape my office and do something wonderful in the kitchen. That's when I challenge a new recipe, create my own shortcuts, tally my efforts, and weigh them against the result: Is it worth the time? Does it live up to my expectations? Will I serve it to my guests? And, here's the clincher: Can I prepare it ahead of time? There is so much the "practicing" hostess has to think of, that figuring out and battling difficult recipes should not be a part of it.

As you begin to master the art of *la belle cuisine,* try to adopt a sense of nonchalance about the whole thing. Like what to do when the roast slips off the serving platter just as you present it to your dinner guests? Of course you know the answer. You have heard stories about Julia Child and Sam Levinson. They are supposed to have quipped smartly while retrieving dinner from the parquet floor: "Excuse me, I'll take this one out and bring in the other roast."

I once tripped over a piece of air on my way to the dinner table bearing a decorated-to-die-for platter with four plump, stuffed, browned-to-perfection Cornish hens nestled in a bed of greens artfully surrounded by pieces of fruit. (Martha Perfect would have been green with envy and split her jeans.) Well, everything flew everywhere: Cornish hens on the wing chasing little kumquats through the air.

"Thank God," I managed to utter dramatically as I retrieved my goodies, "I cooked eight little chicks." I disappeared into the kitchen, clanged and banged things around a bit for effect, rearranged the greenery, replaced the kumquats and spiced crabapples with great precision, and dusted off the hens at top speed. Dinner was delicious! I figured that my house was a lot cleaner than some of the restaurant kitchens I have seen.

Accidents and disasters seem to happen whenever I want to impress — like walking on high heels in a long gown for the first time to meet your date. You make believe you've done that forever and trip over your hem, fall on your face, tear your dress, break a heel, lose your contacts on the shag carpet, and chip a front tooth on your date's Gucci loafers. Horrors! Surely not your finest hour, to put it mildly.

I remember using a brand-new fancy mold that came with a complicated recipe that had more steps than those leading to the Supreme Court building. When it was time to serve the dessert, I dipped and dunked the mold according to instructions. It would NOT unmold. I turned it upside-down one more time and shook it vigorously.

Out came the mold. Before I could position the platter, forty-five ingredients and seventy-nine steps of preparation slipped ever so quietly, without fanfare, into the dark cavern of the garbage disposal. I stood rooted at the sink, staring, trying to reverse the action and not use improper language. I waved the wayward custard-whipped cream-Framboise-fresh raspberry and the other forty-plus precious ingredients a sad farewell and headed for the freezer. My Viennese Nut Torte rested untouched in the "Soup Bone" box in the freezer and saved the day. It pays to be prepared for all eventualities.

Being "cool" or nonchalant about cooking is no different than overcoming the shakes and being "cool" about diapering your brand-new baby the first time, or trying out for an appearance on *Wheel of Fortune*. (Vanna doesn't care!)

The more you practice, the better you'll get. The more organized your kitchen, the better stocked your pantry, the more "ritualistic" your food preparation habits are, the more comfortable, confident and nonchalant you will become about preparing for a dinner party.

At the risk of repeating myself, here I go:

Organization is number one on your list. Here's what to do:

1. Plan your menu.
2. Write down what you want to serve and list the required ingredients on a pad.
3. Check your pantry, refrigerator and freezer and see that everything you need for that particular meal is in the house.
4. Buy fruits and vegetables, meat, fish or poultry fresh the day before your party. Buy your flowers the day before as well, and keep them fresh in ice water, or store them in your refrigerator.
5. If possible, set your table the night before — all but the flowers.
6. Cook ahead the day (or more) before. Remove your dishes from the refrigerator in ample time to let them reach room temperature before reheating or baking.
7. Keep your sink clear and your countertops uncluttered. Wash your utensils as soon as you are through using them. If you have no further need for them, replace them in their customary storage place. When you are done with cooking, tidy up your kitchen.There is nothing more discouraging than

working in a messy place. I wouldn't want to cook either.

8. Work on only one part of your meal at a time. For best results, concentrate on following faithfully the steps for cooking. Some shortcuts just don't work. Sometimes I get in a hurry, or I get over-ambitious and start working on a side dish, dessert or a dip while I'm waiting for something to come to a boil, simmer or sauté. Invariably, I goof and get into trouble. Something boils over, something sticks to the bottom of the pan, something burns to a crisp while I'm "busily saving time." It rarely works for me. Preparing more than one food item at a time can make for more work, add waste, and usually — in my case — bring on a rash of choice Chinese curses. Relax, stare out of the window, go on a mini-vacation to Hawaii, do a little Tai Chi, or sing off-key. The pot will boil in good time and you won't ruin something by doing double duty.

9. Use prepared ingredients whenever available. Some purist culinary aristocrats may turn up their respective noses at this suggestion; so be it. Even though I am sensitive to flavors and tastes, I have not been offended by these ready-to-use products. Just don't use mushroom soup, mother's little hamburger helper, or other fillers and killers.

Who wants to finely chop eight garlic cloves when time is of the essence? Who readily tackles a tough, stringy piece of ginger root and reduces it to "finely chopped" when it is available in a little jar all set to go? Make your own horseradish? No, no. Not I. Most prepared mustards and specialty vinegars are true in flavor and should satisfy even the silkscreened palate of Martha Perfect. There is a good selection of wholesome, tasty marinara sauces on the market (fat-free to boot) to suffice in a pinch and save you from making your own.

Just in case I run out of time while preparing one of those surprise (!) guess-who's-coming-to-Italian-dinner meals, I keep packaged, grated parmesan, as well as romano cheese, on hand, since I don't always have the time to grate cheese on the spot. I firmly believe that shortcuts are healthy, as long as they don't interfere with the quality of a recipe, change the flavor or texture, and Martha Perfect is tending to her periwinkle pigeons and is not looking over your shoulder. It's perfectly okay!

I purchase prepared garlic. I also buy sun-dried tomato or garlic pesto. I don't have the time to chop a bunch of basil and garlic and make my very own pesto.

I rarely chop anything by hand, but use my food processor or hand-held rolling mincer to turn onions, carrots, celery, whatever, into the required coarseness.

What? No fresh mushrooms in the fridge? Stock your pantry with several kinds of canned and dried fungi. Just ask Julia if it's okay. She'll tell you!

Keep frozen vegetables for those emergencies. There are few dishes that would suffer a setback when frozen chopped spinach is substituted for a fresh bunch.

How many times have you reached for milk in your refrigerator and come up with an empty carton in your hand? I have done it enough times to keep several cans of condensed and a package of powdered milk in my pantry, and my sanity intact — after a fashion, that is. For that very reason I always have juices (concentrates) in the freezer — just in case the recipe calls for that one table-spoon of orange juice. My resident would-be marathon runner just drank a full quart of it for breakfast without telling me. He left the "empty" in the refrigerator — an empty promise.

Does anyone know why in the world men put empty cartons back on the shelf and vacated jars of anything back in the refrigerator? (Probably for the same reason they never put a new roll of toilet paper on its holder. Instead, they balance the new supply on the bare cardboard core still in place or, better yet, put it on the floor.) I fully believe that they think of themselves as "neat." Why, oh why, do men — without a blink of a thought — replace the empty cereal box on the pantry shelf? Invariably, next day at breakfast there comes that injured howl accompanied by a few choice words, "*?@!+! We're out of cereal!!!! I wish you'd.... "

Oh, well, I've learned to do a shakedown run in my larders, and have emergency "stuff" on hand. When I first moved into my spacious kitchen, I innocently believed I'd never ever fill its generous cupboards and pantry spaces. Hah! Even if I didn't go to the store for one month, I couldn't fit a bay leaf — anywhere.

If you have a partner who drops his own version of "guess who's coming to dinner" — darling? — on you not so infrequently, then fight back in your own way: be prepared. Pre-cook and freeze a meal or two along with a dessert. I myself am guilty of tending to hand out wild, impulsive invitations of the drop-of-a-hat-you-all-come-to-dinner kind with little time to prepare. For that reason alone, I give a few hours a month to my freezer, to prepare the following menu choices. Nothing has ever gone to waste.

1.   One vegetarian lasagna — eight servings.
2.   One regular lasagna — eight servings.
3.   Crabcakes.
4.   Two to four quarts of marinara sauce.
5.   Spinach crêpes.

6.   Several packages each of linguine, angel hair pasta, ravioli and vegetable tortellini.

7.   Seafood for bouillabaisse or other dishes: one pound each of frozen large shrimp, rock shrimp, and crab meat.

8.   Stock base for curry dishes. (See recipe section.)

9.   Two loaves of herbed garlic bread, foil-wrapped and ready for the oven.

10.   One loaf of herbed cheese bread.

11.   One french baguette.

12.   One lemon cheesecake.

13.   One Viennese nut torte.

This system of having ready-to-heat-and-eat meals on hand is also a terrific safety net in case you are forgetful and/or didn't look at your appointment calendar. Let me tell you what happened to me once — actually twice.

My husband and I had planned to go out to dinner on that particular Saturday night, and I was all dressed, waiting for him to get home, when the doorbell rang. To my (well-hidden) surprise, two couples, fairly new friends all dressed for a little Saturday night celebration, stood at my doorstep, then flowed into the hall with hugs and bearing flowers. Everyone settled comfortably into the living room, full of laughter and ready for a lively evening, while my mind tried to sort out just where and how and when and why and, dear God, who else? Could "they" have made a mistake?

"How come it doesn't smell like ducks roasting in the oven?" inquired one of the men. The ringing of the doorbell came to my temporary rescue. I had a few moments to think of something, or come clean. One more couple joined our little group with cheerful greetings after gently settling a bottle of wine in my arms like a new baby.

Aha! How many in my party of eight? I really had goofed.

I dashed into the kitchen and checked my calendar. Sure enough, there it was:

Dinner, seven p.m. — Bob and Marge, Bill and Sandy, Philip and Veronica. (Serve duck, etc.)

Great! One quick glance into the dining room displayed the table — not set for dinner.

Fortunately, my handy-dandy twelve-year-old daughter was at home. Interrupted by hysterical giggles, I told her of my dilemma and, joining me in another round of wild chuckles, she took over. Lucky for me, Marly had enjoyed hanging around and helping me in the kitchen ever since she was a little girl. Quick and adaptable, she was more than sympathetic to my plight, and charitable enough to save my hide. She also loved a little game of intrigue — after all, she is my daughter.

Not that it would have been a disaster to confess my errors and omissions and take everyone out to dinner on "American Express Green" (Ouch!), but it seemed such an opportunity to see how well I could keep a straight face and put on a meal without missing a beat or two. My China training came in handy.

I made up some lame excuse about the fact that a month without a "D" was not suitable for serving Long Island ducklings. I continued to shade the truth with the story that it was part of my daughter's junior home-ec project to set the table and help with entertaining. She had opted for serving an Italian dinner. I, of course, had given her free rein!

Not waiting for comments and further questions, which would demand another rash of untruths from me, I turned the conversation. By then I was willing to discuss the latest trash from the Sally Jessy grunge show, or the high cost of super-conductor research.

A large lasagna and a generous loaf of garlic bread literally jumped out of the freezer, and straight into the oven. Marly set the table — centerpiece and all — prepared greens for the salad, and she even fixed an appealingly garnished tray with cheeses, crackers and fruit. I popped into the kitchen a few times to lend a hand, but she really didn't need me. I must have done something right! She got an A-plus on her "project."

By the time my husband came home, we were having our second glass of wine, the conversation was flowing, the baked brie was slowly disappearing, and the assuring aroma of garlic and tomatoes promised a delicious meal. Before the unsuspecting host could trip over the assortment of cars, Marly heard him turn into the driveway and ran out to warn him of the comedy playing out in the living room. Great daughter!

We had a lovely evening, good food, good company. Years later, I confessed my sins to my friends. All they remembered was the fact that they had a great time, and not what they ate! We all had a good laugh.

I did the same brilliant trip again some years later, except that I didn't have a daughter at home to haul me out of the hole I had dug for myself. This time my husband was at home and filled wine glasses and passed nuts and pretzels, while I headed for the freezer.

I quickly retrieved a loaf of the herbed cheese bread, a container with my curry base, one pound of shrimp, one pound of rock shrimp, and a package of scallops. I ran hot water over the plastic container with the curry base, dumped it all in a dutch oven, and put it on the stove on medium-low. Threw the bread in the oven at 400 degrees, and the seafood on "Defrost" in the microwave.

My friends (a different group) were a bit suspicious that time, when I disappeared into the dining room and kitchen more often and stayed longer than I ever did. I don't know if anyone noticed that I was setting the table, throwing things in the oven, dishing out the seven condiments accompanying any respectable curry dish, and fixing a green salad. At least I had it all in the house.

It took no time to assemble the curry, cook the (minute) rice, reach for the condiments and have dinner on the table at just about the usual time. This time I confessed over coffee and dessert. I did it during a pleasant round of Two Truths and a Lie and was not caught! That's one for me!

That's why I always have two kinds of desserts — whole or in part — (see dessert section) stashed away in the freezer in a large carton marked "Soup Bones." Nobody ever bothered to look inside that box — soup bones do not make good snacks. As a matter of fact, the hiding place was so safe that I kept my jewelry and my citizenship papers right next to the Viennese Nut Torte. In a hurry one day, I made a big mistake and asked my husband to bring me the "Soup Bone" carton from the downstairs freezer as I was getting ready for guests.

When he saw me lift out his favorite lemon cheese cake — whole, perfect and untouched — a twice-wicked ah-ha! kind of light went on in his eyes. I knew I had just given him the keys to my Fort Knox of desserts. Soon after that, I announced in a casual by-the-by chatty sort of way that I was collecting salmon heads and fish bones to make a quart or two of fish stock for some of my seafood dishes. My collection would be stored in the freezer in a box marked, "Fish Bones," what else?

Get in the habit of pre-cooking a main dish or two, preparing a loaf or two of garlic bread, herbed cheese bread, and a couple of desserts "for the freezer." Just knowing that you're ahead of the hosting game will make you feel a bit uppity — on top of the world and ready for unexpected guests. These treasures in your freezer are the best insurance against the jitters when you know that guests are coming. Just get the parsley; dinner is done!

You can fool a heck of a lot of people into believing that you're a real whiz kid in the kitchen department and the reincarnation of Pearl Mesta in the drawing room if you learn how to plan, get organized and be prepared. Someone once told me: "When hell freezes over ... ice skate!"

I've done my share of skating, and I'm getting better at it all the time!

Chapter Nine

Open the Door and Welcome the World

*Oh, the fun of arriving at a house and feeling
the spirit that tells you that you're going to have
a good time.*
— *Mark Hampton*

There are gatherings where the host and hostess invite everyone who has ever crossed their paths, no matter how brief the encounter. More often than not, these big shindigs are held for no better reason than to "pay back" and "get it over with." Movie stars give parties for several hundred of their most intimate friends. International socialites rent whole cities to accommodate their guests for that chic "little" bash. A party like that demands the talents of a census taker just to know who's who, who's not, and how does she spell her current name?

Elsa Maxwell once said, "The cocktail party is easily the worst invention since castor oil." I have to agree with her.

It's my turn to be nervous and shaky when an invitation announcing a cocktail-buffet, open-house, house warming, come-as-you-are, or what-have-you party arrives in the mail. Someone referred to a cocktail buffet as "grazing on the hoof in overheated and overcrowded conditions." So be it. When that chilling announcement of an impendent mass feeding event arrives in my mailbox, it's my turn to change my name, buy a wig and leave town.

I'm not crazy about crowds. I have never been overly fond of balancing a drink, a plate and inane conversation with total strangers, while trying to lean against a "wall" for support that turns out to be a person. Sooner or later someone invariably loses control over his dip and chip, which lands on the front of my dress. The culprit then adds insult to injury and attempts to remove the accident with the remains of his scotch and the cute paper napkin, dripping purple ink. So much for that kind of togetherness.

Have you noticed how it can take the better part of an evening just to find the hostess in the crowd? I have learned to say Hello, Goodbye and Thank You all at the same time the moment I catch her attention, knowing full well I won't get another chance.

One of my favorite comments regarding the pitfalls of large cocktail parties is attributed to the unerringly witty Noel Coward. Upon entering a socialite's swank Manhattan apartment and surveying the humming, buzzing crowd in a smoke-filled drawing room, he turned to his hostess and quipped, "Had I known you invited all your friends, I would have worn my armor."

Don't you wish you'd said that! That dear man must have known that it is easier to remove chip-n'-dip from a suit of armor than from a tender silken garment.

I understand that a cocktail buffet satisfies a variety of purposes — like paying back the So-and-Sos, using up every name on his and hers rolodexes — testing how many people the house can hold without causing a shift in the foundation — or — conducting a survey on how far a gallon of bean dip stretches and watching the sliced ham curl up and die. Ugh!

The cause for the event may even be nothing more serious than to support someone's dubious choice for dogcatcher or promote the right to life of the tsetse fly. The party also offers a great opportunity to use those cunning little paper napkins that match the witty invitations straight from the shelves of the neighborhood "Hellmark" store.

On those rare occasions when I'm all out of excuses — I'm not hiding out in a bungalow on Saba — and I am being dragged to a cocktail buffet in chains, I'm doomed to run into total strangers who insist on having met me before — even if it turns out to be in another life. When it's all over — who cares? Have another go at the bean dip and the ham!

These huge you-all-come gatherings invariably attract their share of hardcore, silk-suited networkers who attempt to sell anything from parimutuel insurance, a safety net for bungee jumping, mutual funds in Zimbabwe, wetland real estate, new-age vitamins, or a cruise on the *Titanic*. The not-so-innocent cocktail buffet has become the vehicle for people to promote their services and products to the beat of the thump-bumping of a rock band from the CD player. The only good thing about all this is that the house is so noisy that I can only hear snatches of the conversation. I've dropped my collection of business cards on the floor, and there's no room to bend down to retrieve them — and it is time to leave.

That's not entertaining, that's torture on a paper plate.

We all have been there … done that. I did it. I gave "big shindigs" a few times too often. No need to tell you how the house looked the next day, nor the wet rings that added additional distress to the already distressed antiques. If you're lucky, you'll end up with only a few unclaimed coats and jackets (never in your size and color), and no more than one or two guests left staggering up from the lower level of your house the next morning, eager to find out where they are and why. But then you've already been through all that. So why ask for more of the same?

I have made it a rule not to invite more people than I can comfortably seat. I hold to that for a dinner party, a kitchen dinner, or an informal gathering for wine and nibbles. No matter what, I always seem to end up with my favorite number of six and no more than eight people.

If you'd like to get your feet wet before your first dinner party, try entertaining for just "drinks and tidbits" — a civilized "cocktail party." Invite the number of people (congenial) you can group with ease around your coffee table. Serve a few simple nibbles (see recipe section). Putting on something as uncomplicated as this will let you test your talent for mixing personalities, and offers you a chance to pick and choose the tone and mood you wish to create. Fresh flowers, a few candles to flatter the mood, and background music (kids with a sitter far from the scene) are still in order. Colorful cloth napkins will lend a touch of grace to even a casual affair. I like grace better than class — don't you?

Your guests will leave with a warm glow and a few memories of a "civilized" evening without having to get Freddy off the chandelier or stopping Mabel in her rayon mini from reading palms inside the fireplace among the glowing embers.

In comparison to large parties, there is nothing more appealing to me and, as it turns out, more than welcomed by most people, than an evening spent in good conversation in the company of a few. To a great extent, the fabulous days of the Salon are gone. Those cherished gatherings of poetry readings and philosophical excursions beyond the limits of the mind have vanished. Time for leisure and contemplation is being consumed by the accelerated demands of the fast-lane, fast-food syndrome in which many of us seem to be caught. Poetry got lost on the Internet. The art of letter writing is being reduced to messages on e-mail, and — to the great horror of dear Miss Manners — faxed thank-you notes are about to become the order of the day.

Listening to wisdom on tapes, attending lecturers via television cable conferences, reading personal greetings on the cold, grey screen of your personal computer may be admirable technology, but it will never replace the human touch, the spontaneity of quick laughter, the eye-to-eye contact, and the warmth of a hug.

From Fargo to Manhattan, crisscrossing the country, people are committed to keeping up, becoming high-tech savvy, being successful and staying on target to meet their five-year goals in three. Considering these facts, it seems to me more important than ever that some of our few leisure moments become a sort of fly-me-to-the-moon kind of a time of memorable delights. Society continually shifts its moods and tastes as it rushes here and there looking for something new and different. But, more often than not, we reach back into the past for what was enduring — more graceful and private, more elegant and more purposeful than what perhaps could be called old-fashioned. Coco Chanel said it years ago as she compared lifestyles to fashion: "Good taste and good manners never go out of style."

Perhaps we can bring back bits of our rich past and the ways of the Salon, and create for ourselves and our friends moments that take us beyond the ordinary and away from the oh-so impersonal bleeps and blips of superhighway on-line madness.

A small gathering of fun people, a no-fuss meal, a setting that promotes a degree of festivity, and a brisk, lively exchange of ideas can do just that. Do it, you'll love it!

Just think of what you expect from an evening out. It really means time spent away from the ordinary, and doing something beyond the extraordinary. If you go to the theater or a concert, if you attend an opera or a lecture, or see a movie, you are taken out of your daily routine and transported into another world. You can do that in your home for your guests and for yourself. You set the stage. You supervise the script. You direct the play. You'll have a grand time and your guests will take the magic you've created home with them. It's all worth the work, the time and the expense. It's magic.

You might be among those who create a place for themselves and their friends to celebrate the return of a certain simple elegance — moments of intellectual challenges, spiritual camaraderie, along with the charm and wit of the Salon of a more graceful time.

So, what's there to be nervous about? You know the magic words:

Let's have dinner — soon!

Is tomorrow too soon?

Chapter Ten
All About the Menus

Chef: Any cook who curses in French.
– Henry Beard and Roy McKie

The menus and the interchangeable side dishes in this section are true-and-tried recipes, and if you follow the instructions for preparation faithfully, they won't fail you. In the course of reading current food magazines, I realize that, like anything else in the world today, food tastes try to be trendy, nouvelle, chic and healthy. But not so nouvelle are the kind of dishes that are claiming the limelight of chefsmanship at the present time.

Among several kinds of "yesterday" foods to recently gain attention, the humble meatloaf is at the top of the list. Also on the comeback trail are scalloped potatoes, thick slices of a down-home, gravy-rich pot roast; and, Southern or otherwise, fried chicken minus the benefits of exotic herbs, tropical salsa or garlic basting. The pork roast, banned and cursed with having "too many fat grams," returns in the guise of "that other white meat." Pork has once more become a respectable and très chic main course, for which chefs have concocted a rash of gravies and sauces to grace this recently eschewed too-fat-for-me meat. Personally, I had not noticed that all the above had been un-chic. I just hadn't thought of them — not that I don't like meatloaf.

But I'm not as chic and healthy as one might think.

I believe that good food is good food — chic, old or nouvelle. And if you want to be a confident hostess and able to fully rely on what comes out of your kitchen, then — trendy or not — prepare only those recipes you have learned to do with ease and are certain of their outcome. Don't fuss and worry, relax — what the heck! Remember, your friends are coming to see *you* — enjoy them!

Good food ... should not be regarded as a poison, a medicine, or a talisman. It should be eaten and enjoyed.
– From a report of the
National Academy of Sciences

Now we come to the much-discussed and, for some, worrisome aspects of food and health!

We have become more conscious about the consumption of fat and calories in the last few years. However, not always do opinions and findings agree with each other. One day a group of food gurus decides fat is bad for us — unless, of course, you are an Eskimo, live in Alaska, and your steady diet consists of salmon and blubber.

No sooner are you looking for an igloo in the North than you'll hear findings to the contrary. Recent test results revealed that not enough fat in the diet makes nervous wrecks out of rats and, thus deprived, these little critters stopped all romantic activities. Well, we can't have that. You know whatever happens to rats eventually happens to our best friends and, most probably, to you and me.

Then I came across a most comforting thought from another "reputable" source (one of those late-night talk shows in search of sensational material), which pointed out that even if we adhere to every fatless, low-sugar, low-life health rule, we'd only live six months longer than those fat lovers with a sweet tooth. Shucks! Now I ask you, is it worth it?

If, however, you remain firm about your fat-free convictions, choose recipes that are originally designed to be prepared without fatty ingredients — then you won't be disappointed if the results don't meet your expectations. Some people insist that adding lots of herbs makes up for the loss of the flavor produced by fat. But just how much parsley, rosemary and thyme can a butter cookie hold?

I'm all for healthy; being cautious is admirable. Being overly concerned is like installing a safety net on the basement ceiling — just in case the first-floor living room caves in. Enjoy life, live a lot!

In order to appease both sides of the fatty issue, I have cut down considerably on some of the fat-containing ingredients in most of the recipes in this book, but I have left enough of that wonderful stuff in to retain the intended flavor and texture of the food.

Let's face it: once or twice a week, nothing can hurt you. How often do you go out to dinner? How frequently do you dive head first into a bowl of whipped cream? How many times a week do you entertain at dinner and serve rich food? Everyone can adhere to being fat-less and taste-less, cautious and healthy for five or even six days a week. I fully believe that on the sixth day God already considered taking it easy, and on the seventh day, he rested. So don't ruin your dinner party by worrying about a few extra calories and fat grams. Enjoy yourself and be "light and healthy" Monday through Friday. But not tonight, Josephine! Not tonight!

I don't guarantee the outcome of a recipe if you insist on substituting yogurt, soybean milk, no-fat sour cream or mayonnaise, tofu or other fat-free-taste-free ersatz products. They don't work; I've tried. I watch what we eat when we are by ourselves at home. I keep the lid on the sour cream, the whipped cream, and the half and half. Butter is miserly rationed out, mayonnaise is barely whisked over a piece of bread on the rare occasions we have a sandwich. Rich salad dressings are replaced with lemon juice or a light vinaigrette. Desserts stay in the box labeled "Fish Bones for Stock" in the freezer. Fresh fruit, sorbet or baked apples, and fruit compote take the place of calorie-laden goodies.

I don't approach cooking with a fat gram counter in one hand and a cup of low-life tofu in the other. You don't have to either. But if you're concerned about health issues, plan your meals for balance. If you use a rich sauce for the main course, the vegetable will only get a squeeze of lemon juice along with a touch of parsley, or a fine herb for seasoning. Prepare the accompanying rice, pasta or potato dish with only a modest amount of butter, olive oil, cheese or cream. But don't be too stingy or you'll lose the flavor of the food you're preparing. If, on the other hand, you wish to throw all caution to the wind for that one special night — enjoy the feast; everybody will love it, too. (Also, don't tell all — keep a secret or two. A few fat grams more or less on occasion won't interfere with anyone's chances of winning the lottery of Life Eternal.)

Hints and Tips

Next, plan your menu to fit the season as well as the occasion.

Serve light meals during hot summer nights. Save that hearty shepherd's pie or pork roast with gnocchi for a cooler day. Instead, prepare lemon-grilled breast of chicken Florentine with tiny parsley potatoes, or a poached or grilled salmon fillet with fresh fruit salsa, and herbed rice preceded by elegant wild greens enhanced by bits of ripe julienned pears and a tangy, fruity vinaigrette (see recipe). These are satisfying meals, but light and breezy for hot-weather dining.

Use in-season vegetables; they are more flavorful than at any other time of the year and are economical to boot.

If you know you will have a slightly crowded dinner table, serve a main course that doesn't require a knife for cutting. Your guests might not have the elbow room to wield a knife and a fork.

Always let refrigerated and (some) frozen foods* reach room temperature before cooking, reheating or baking. (*There are some dishes that are intended to go from freezer to oven or microwave — follow instructions.)

When you prepare vegetables ahead of time for serving as appetizers, keep them in ice-cold water in the refrigerator to retain their crispness.

If you plan to use fresh pea pods in a green salad, or for nibbles on a vegetable tray, keep them refrigerated in a bowl of ice water and they remain crisp and crunchy.

You can fix your salad greens in the morning of the dinner party. If you wrap the selected greens in moist paper towels and place the packet in a plastic bag, they will be perfect when you're ready to toss and serve your salad. Chill the salad plates in the freezer for a while. It makes your salad even better.

Prepare tomatoes or cucumbers you might want to serve along with your salad early in the day, sprinkle sparingly with your favorite vinaigrette, place in airtight containers, and refrigerate till dinnertime.

Finely slice red onions for your salad, place them in a dish with water, add one teaspoon sugar, cover and refrigerate for several hours; drain well and toss with greens. The onion slices will be crisp and have lost some of their sting.

The more chores you can do ahead, the less you're apt to get nervous about entertaining.

When a recipe recommends: stir constantly…they're not kidding you. I have challenged that advice more times than I want to admit, and as a result I have trashed a few pots in the process.

Look for additional hints and tips with each recipe, and remember:

"Food imaginatively and lovingly prepared, and eaten in good company, warms the being with something more than the mere intake of calories." So stated Marjorie Kinnan Rawlins. Dear Marjorie — you probably know all about her.

Kitchen Dinner Menus

Beautiful soup, so rich and green,
Waiting in a hot tureen!
Who for such dainties would not stop!
Soup of the evening, beautiful soup.
– Lewis Carroll

There is no reason why the following menus I have named kitchen dinners couldn't come to the dining-room table. The only reason I call them "Kitchen Dinners" is because they are one-container meals and, secondly, two of the recipes require last-minute touches which you can do while your guests are at the table and in your sight. You'll be able to visit with them, cook at the same time, prepare the portions, and serve in one fell swoop.

Also, the idea of such a dinner may help the nervous hostess to get started entertaining friends. "A Little Kitchen Dinner" may sound sound less demanding, quite casual, and a lot less threatening to the nervous system.

Your kitchen table can be set in enchanting ways, immediately creating a festive mood that helps celebrate the occasion. Try one of these combinations:

Along with a few candles on the center of your kitchen table, cluster several bedding plants in clay pots (pansies, geraniums, petunias or primroses), which you can later plant in your flowerbed, or:

Fill a large bowl full of fruit and vegetables, intersperse with fresh flowers in glass vials (get vials from your florist), and place several votive candles in their midst, or:

Place a container with daisies in the center of a basket — lined and puffed up with colorful napkins or bright, cheery kitchen towels.

If your light fixture over the kitchen table is too bright, put in smaller bulbs for that evening or, better yet, install a dimmer.

Use bright kitchen towels for placemats and napkins. Use colorful napery, linens — anything from gingham and plaids to homespun and fringed — unusual napkin rings, and colored stemware to create a homey, casual, country atmosphere. Or, use accessories to complement your kitchen decor — whatever the style.

You'd be surprised how comfortable your guests will be, and how stressless the event is for you. You're in your kitchen — relax, nothing can go wrong. Your guests will have a grand time. You'll probably have to pry them away from the table with a crowbar, bundle them in their coats and send them home!

Hors d'Oeuvres

For the past several years, I have kept pre-dinner nibbles at a minimum and tailored the amount I prepare to my guests' appetites — those I know about, that is. I am not very original about serving hors d'oeuvres simply because I don't take the time for putting together a tray of goodies to resemble a Monet painting. That's for caterers and cruise-ship chefs. Years ago, I would spend hours on stuffing and spreading and filling, creating, decorating all sorts of fancy morsels. I don't do that anymore. I keep it simple and prevent wasting time and food.

(Can you think of anything more "dead" than a tray of yesterday's hors d'oeuvres? You'll never see a master's still life of old avocado dip, tired little sandwiches, and soggy pastry shells filled with grey/green moss entitled "The Party's Over.")

I have simplified my life. The following tidbits have become my "regulars." They require little work, are prepared ahead of time, and are made appealing by placing them on trays decked out in greenery, a few flowers, small bunches of red and green grapes, and a few strawberries tossed here and there for color.

Garnishes

What with everything it takes to get dinner on the table in an "unhurried, cool and collected" way — making it look so-o-o easy — don't push to make your "presentation" rival that of Chef Haricot or Martha Perfect. Remember what Julia said when eyeing a heavily decorated tray of appetizers: "It's so beautifully arranged on the plate — you know someone's fingers have been all over it."

I don't have the time to play Picasso and paint a still life with roasted red pepper sauces, enhanced by a fine dusting of dried parsley. I keep it simple — simple things work.

The few things I use to make food look appealing are quick, inexpensive and effective. Everything I plan to use for garnishing has been prepared and is on the kitchen counter cut or sliced, wrapped and ready to place. Here are some of the things I use:

Chives: A few sprigs of chives crisscrossed on a serving of meat or fish.

Lemons and Limes: Thinly sliced for layering, or slashed for creating curls.

Parsley: Italian parsley (flat leaves) makes a more unique garnish than regular parsley.

Kale: Great for lining large platters to present fowl, fish or sliced meats and cheeses.

Collard Greens: For dressing up hors d'oeuvres trays, or used sparingly on dinner plates.

Kumquats: Nice to have on hand for fall and winter entertaining; colorful and unique.

Fresh Herbs: Sprigs of fresh herbs look great, but be sure the flavor of the herb doesn't clash with spices used in the meal you're serving. I am especially careful with cilantro — it really isn't to everyone's taste.

Sprigs of rosemary or thyme are great for pork and lamb, and dill weed seems to be wed to fish. (They must have made their appearance on the planet at the same time!)

A cluster of fresh, fragrant basil leaves is a welcome garnish for any Italian dish, from lasagna to linguine and all your pasta-pasta.

The feathery green stems of the fennel root (anise) is pretty and goes with everything!

Fruit: Kiwi fruit, a small cluster of frosted grapes, a fresh strawberry with stem on, all add texture and color to a dinner plate.

Lemon Leaves: This hardy, heart-shaped leaf (available at your florist for just a few cents) is great for garnishing hors d'oeuvres platters, around pâté or bowls of dip, and even on the dinner plate. Scrubbed clean, it makes a fine resting place for pats of butter.

Flowers: If you want to use flowers for decorations, remember that pansies and nasturtiums are so-called "edibles." Anything that smells like a geranium or a marigold is banned from the dinner table — not unlike bad manners.

There's really no end to things available for garnishing; just don't make it a stumbling block, a chore that adds work and demands precious time — a tiny bit of something goes a long way!

Appetizers, Nibbles — Whatevers

Cheese Pimiento Mushroom Melt

Chicken Liver Pâté

Chutney *Brie en Brioche*

Crisp Vegetables with Tangy Red Dip

Flaky Pesto Pinwheels

Hot Artichoke Crabmeat Dip

Fresh Tomato Relish

All but the Pinwheels can be served with toasted French bread rounds or Crostini.

The Menus
Kitchen Dinners

Farmer's Beef-Vegetable Soup
Tossed Greens with Chardonnay Vinaigrette
Cornbread *
Apple Walnut Crisp

Shepherd's Pie
Tomato Cucumber Salad in Vinaigrette
Crusty Sourdough Bread
with Artichoke-Pesto Butter
Lemon Mousse

Ham and Noodle Casserole
Spinach Salad with Mandarin Slices
Toasted French Rounds
Blueberry Hazelnut Crumble

Texas Black Bean Soup
Tossed Greens with Pickled Fresh Vegetable Relish
Raspberry Vinaigrette
Crisp Hot French Baguettes
Peach Cobbler

* packaged

Winter Holiday

Roasted Cornish Game Hens with
Rob's Wild Rice Cranberry-Almond Stuffing
Orange-Parsley Buttered Brussels Sprouts and Carrots
Curried Fruit
Cucumbers Emilie
Cheese Puff Dinner Rolls
Lemon Cheesecake

Leg of Lamb with Moroccan Sauce
Mashed Parsnip Potatoes
Sliced Cucumbers with Sour Cream-Chive Dressing
Cornbread *
Viennese Nut Torte

* packaged

Summer Nights
Al Fresco Dining

Gazpacho Tureen
Mandarin Orange, Grapefruit Sections and
Persian Melon on Boston Bibb Lettuce with
Raspberry Vinaigrette
Crisp French Baguette with Red Currant Butter
Last-Minute Trifle

Summer Picnic

For that perfect family reunion, paint-the-barn,
smell-the-roses kind of garden/patio dinner

Cold Sliced Lemon/Teriyaki Chicken Breasts
Chilled Salmon with Dill-Mayonnaise
Mango Salsa
Garden Potato Salad
Green Peas and Water Chestnuts Salad
Fruit Salad Medley with Lemonade Dressing
Pickled Mushrooms, Cornichons, Olives, and
Artichokes Tray
Chunks of Sourdough Bread
Silesian Walnut Pastry Crescents

Seafood Menus

Grilled Salmon Fillets
Mango Salsa
Pasta Primavera
Asparagus on Tossed Greens with
Raspberry Vinaigrette
Crostini
Trifle

Indian Shrimp Curry
with Seven Condiments
White Steamed Rice *
Polka-Dot Vegetable Salad
Breadsticks
Death by Chocolate Mousse Cake

Linguine with Rock Shrimp in Green Clam Sauce
Romaine Lettuce and Julienne Pears
with Chardonnay Vinaigrette
Herb-Garlic Bread
Apple Cheesecake

* packaged

Bouillabaisse
Wild Greens with Asparagus Bundles
with Raspberry Vinaigrette
Crostini
Apple Walnut Crisp

Northwest Crab Cakes
Grilled Stuffed Tomatoes
Spanakopita
Hot French Bread
Black Forest Trifle

Pasta Perfecto
For All Your Mama-Nanno Nights

Lasagna Bolognese
Cæsar Salad
Parmesan Garlic Bread
Lemon Cheesecake

Vegetarian Lasagna
Spinach Salad
Crostini
Berry Cobbler with Ginger Whipped Cream

Meatballs Marinara with Linguine
Tossed Greens with
Chardonnay Vinaigrette
Crostini
Debbie's Lemon Baba

Dinner Menus

Chicken Paprikash
Herbed Mushroom Rice
No-Fail Broccoli Soufflé
Wild Greens with Raspberry Vinaigrette
Cheese Puff Dinner Rolls
Strawberry Fool

Honey Chicken Surprise
Rice Pilaf *
Asparagus with Lemon Butter
Cornbread *
Viennese Nut Torte

Lemon Chicken Florentine
Petite Parsley Potatoes
Grilled Stuffed Tomatoes
Sliced Cucumbers with Sour Cream-Chive Dressing
Herb-Garlic Bread
Night and Day Chocolate Mousse
on Hazelnut Meringues

* packaged

Mediterranean Chicken
Pasta Primavera
Spinach Salad with Mandarin Slices
Parmesan Garlic Bread
Debbie's Lemon Baba

Veal Marsala
Gnocchi *
Brussels Sprouts and Carrots with Orange-Parsley Butter
Asparagus on Tossed Greens with
Chardonnay Vinnaigrette
Herb-Garlic Bread
Viennese Nut Torte

Beef Stroganoff
Steamed Rice
No-Fail Spinach Soufflé
Wild Greens with Cider Vinaigrette
Crusty Sourdough Bread
with Artichoke-Pesto Butter
Peach Walnut Crisp

* packaged

Vegetarian Delight

Crêpes* - Mushroom-Spinach Stuffed
Grilled Stuffed Tomatoes
Tossed Greens with Chardonnay Vinaigrette
Apple Cheesecake

*Other options for crêpes fillings:
Ground Beef with Mushrooms (see recipes)
Chicken Ragoufin
Seafood Hollandaise

Appetizers

Cheese Pimiento Mushroom Melt

1 pound sharp cheddar cheese, shredded
1 (8-ounce) jar diced pimientos, drained
1 (8-ounce) can mushrooms, drained
3/4 cup mayonnaise
1/2 teaspoon garlic powder
3 dashes Tabasco sauce
6 to 8 English or Australian muffins, halved

In a large bowl, combine first six ingredients. (Keeps in refrigerator for as long as three days.) Bring to room temperature.

Preheat oven to 350 degrees. Place muffin halves on foil-covered cookie sheet and bake until slightly crisp, about 10 minutes. Remove from oven.

Spread evenly with 3 tablespoons of cheese mixture; replace on cookie sheet. Set broiler on high. Place muffins in middle of oven and broil until cheese mixture bubbles and turns golden brown. Keep an eye on the muffins — do not let them burn! To serve as hors d'oeuvres, cut muffins into bite sized pieces.

For variety and change of flavor, you can add 8 ounces of fresh crabmeat, or 8 ounces of salad shrimp or 1/2 cup pecan pieces. It makes a delicious (quick too!) luncheon fare, served with a green salad.

Serves 6 to 8

Chicken Liver Pâté

1-1/2 pounds chicken livers, trimmed
1/2 cup flour (to coat chicken livers)
1 large onion, sliced fine
8 large mushrooms, sliced fine
4 tablespoons margarine
1/2 envelope unflavored gelatin
2 tablespoons brandy (Apple brandy is one of my keep-on-
    hand liquors.)
1 tablespoon lemon juice

Soften gelatin in lemon juice and brandy, microwave
for 15 seconds or until gelatin is dissolved; set aside.

Sauté onions in margarine until translucent. Add
chicken livers; brown for 4 minutes on each side. Remove
livers and onions to paper towels to drain excess fat.

Place liver and onions in blender; add gelatin mixture
and mushrooms. Blend till smooth. Pack in plastic
container, cover and chill at least 4 hours. Unmold;
arrange on greens.

Serve with crackers or bread rounds and cornichons.

Serves 8 to 12

Chutney Brie en Brioche

1 sheet puff pastry
1 (12-ounce) wheel of brie
2 tablespoons chutney
1 egg
1 tablespoon water

Defrost pastry dough. Roll out sheet to measure about 10x16 inches. Position wheel of brie in center of puff pastry sheet. Top brie evenly with layer of chutney of your choice; mine is apple-pear jalapeño. Bring dough around cheese to make a tight wrap, pinching seams to fuse (trim off excess*); leave no part of cheese uncovered. Seal well!
(Keeps in the refrigerator for as long as two days.)
Preheat oven to 375 degrees. Before baking, apply egg wash: Beat egg with water. Apply to pastry with brush. Bake for 20 to 30 minutes or until golden brown. Cool for 20 minutes before serving.
Serve with French bread rounds or crackers.

Serves 6 to 8

*Reserve balance of dough; cut into strips, twist and bake on a cookie sheet until golden brown.

Crisp Vegetables with
Tangy Red Dip

1/3 cup sugar
1/3 cup catsup
2 tablespoons olive oil
1/4 cup red wine vinegar
1 small onion, finely chopped
juice of 1/2 lemon
1 teaspoon paprika
1 teaspoon pepper
(salt optional)

Place all ingredients in food processor. Blend till smooth. Cover and chill. (Keeps up to two weeks in refrigerator.)

Serve as a dip with raw vegetables. (Also works as a tangy dressing for tossed greens.)

Flaky Pesto Pinwheels

12 ounces cream cheese, softened
1 cup parmesan cheese, grated
2 green onions with tops, finely chopped
2 tablespoons prepared pesto
2 sheets puff pastry

Blend first four ingredients quickly in food processor until smooth. Roll out pastry sheets to measure 10 x16-inch rectangles. Divide cheese mixture; spread evenly over both sheets. Roll tightly; wrap in plastic. Freeze. (Keeps in freezer for up to 3 months.)

When ready to bake, thaw until easily cut. Cut into pinwheels about 1/4-inch thick. Bake at 375 degrees for 12 minutes.

One roll serves 12

Fresh Tomato Relish

4 tomatoes, seeded and chopped
2 tablespoons finely chopped sweet onion
2 tablespoons chopped fresh basil
2 teaspoons balsamic vinegar
2 teaspoons olive oil

Mix all ingredients thoroughly. Cover and refrigerate. (Will stay fresh for four days.)

Serve with crostini. Delicious and light.

Hot Artichoke Crabmeat Dip

1-1/2 teaspoons olive oil
1/2 medium red pepper, seeded and finely chopped
1 (14-ounce) can artichoke hearts, drained and chopped
1 cup mayonnaise
1/2 cup parmesan cheese, grated
1/4 cup green onions, thinly sliced
1 tablespoon worcestershire sauce
1 tablespoon jalapeño pepper, finely chopped (optional)
2 teaspoons lemon juice
8 ounces fresh crabmeat, drained and picked over
1/3 cup slivered almonds

Sauté pepper in olive oil about 5 minutes. Transfer pepper to a large bowl.

Add all other ingredients, except almonds, and combine. Transfer mixture to 8-inch quiche or pie pan with 1-1/2-inch-high sides. Spread evenly. Sprinkle with slivered almonds.

Bake at 375 degrees for 30 minutes, or until golden brown. Serve warm with french bread rounds or garlic bread.

Serves 6 to 8

Breads and Spreads

About Breads

I buy all the breads I serve. There's barely a corner in our cities that doesn't have a fine bakery or stores carrying good breads, from sourdough cannonballs to crusty loaves, to long and slim baguettes.

There are breads with the flavor of dark, rich molasses, fragrant textures, herbed, garlicked. Loaves with bits of hazelnuts and oats. On and on, the parade of breads is endless and delicious; it requires no more work than bringing home the bread!

Just remember the differences in breads: French breads are crusty and of lighter texture, not unlike their country of origin. Sourdough breads are usually tougher in crust and denser in texture, not unlike the rest of the world.

Most breads are tastier when served warm and crisp. Heat breads at 375 degrees for 5 minutes; slice and serve.

Artichoke-Pesto Butter

4 ounces soft unsalted butter
1 tablespoon prepared garlic pesto
4 tablespoons artichoke hearts, finely chopped

Combine all ingredients in blender until thoroughly mixed. Place in serving container to store. Chill lightly; do not let it get *too* firm. Serve at room temperature with french bread, rolls, etc.

Serves 8 to 12

Cheese Puff Dinner Rolls

1 package Parker House rolls (bake and serve)
4 tablespoons butter
1/2 cup parmesan cheese, grated

Cut rolls in half. Melt butter; add parmesan cheese and blend thoroughly.

Quickly dip rolls in butter mixture and place on foil-lined baking sheet. Drizzle remaining butter mixture on rolls.

Prepare in the morning; cover. When ready to bake, uncover and bake in 375-degree oven for 15 to 20 minutes, or until golden brown.

Serves 6 to 8

Crostini

6 ounces butter or olive oil
1 teaspoon minced garlic, or 1 teaspoon garlic pesto
1 French baguette, cut in 1/4-inch rounds, or sliced at an
    angle

Preheat oven to 375 degrees.

Melt butter and garlic. Brush bread rounds generously
with melted butter, one side only; arrange on ungreased
foil-lined cookie sheet.

Bake for 15 minutes or until golden brown. Wrap foil
around bread rounds; place in serving basket or tray. Cover
with napkin. Serve.

Serves 6 to 8

Herb-Garlic Bread

8 ounces butter
1 teaspoon prepared garlic
1/2 teaspoon rosemary, dried
1/2 teaspoon thyme, dried
1 loaf French bread, halved lengthwise

Place butter, garlic and spices in bowl; melt in microwave for 1 minute. Drizzle evenly over halves of bread. Join halves.

Wrap tightly in foil and store. (Can be frozen for up to 4 weeks.) Bake at 450 degrees for 25 minutes. Reduce heat to 350 degrees, open foil and spread halves; bake for 8 minutes or turn on broiler to brown bread halves. Watch it! I've broiled my bread to charcoal once or twice.

Parmesan Garlic Bread

8 ounces butter
1 teaspoon prepared garlic
1 loaf French bread, halved lengthwise
1/2 cup parmesan cheese

Place butter and garlic in bowl; melt in microwave for 1 minute. Drizzle evenly over halves of bread. Sprinkle with parmesan, join halves.

Wrap tightly in foil and store. (Can be frozen for up to 4 weeks.) Bake, still wrapped, at 425 degrees for 25 minutes. Reduce heat to 350 degrees, open foil and spread halves; bake for 8 minutes or turn on broiler to brown bread halves. Watch it! I've broiled my bread to charcoal once or twice.

Red Currant Butter

4 ounces soft butter
3 tablespoons red currant jelly

Combine ingredients in blender until thoroughly mixed. Place in serving container to store. Chill.

Serve at room temperature with french bread, rolls, or bread of your choice.

Desserts

Apple Cheesecake

This dessert may take a bit longer to prepare, but it's worth it.

Crust:
4 ounces butter
1/3 cup sugar
1 cup flour
Filling:
12 ounces soft cream cheese
1/4 cup sugar
1 whole egg
1 teaspoon vanilla
2 tablespoons lemon juice
Topping:
3 Granny Smith apples, peeled, quartered, sliced thinly
1 package *Oetker's* Glaze*, follow directions

Crust: Melt butter; add sugar and flour. Work with fingertips into a soft ball. You can stop here, wrap dough in plastic, and keep at room temperature until the next day.

Filling: Mix cream cheese, sugar, egg, vanilla and lemon juice. You can stop here; cover. Store at room temperature.

Topping: Let apple slices come to a quick boil in 1/4 cup water. Simmer on low heat for 3 minutes. Drain; reserve liquid. Cover and store at room temperature.

The next day: Preheat oven to 400 degrees. Pat dough into an 8-inch springform pan; build up sides to create a 1-1/2 -inch rim. Fill evenly with cream cheese mixture. Overlap apple slices in a concentric pattern on top of cheese filling. Crimp down pastry rim to align evenly with apple topping.

Bake 10 minutes at 400 degrees, then 25 minutes at 350 degrees. Remove from oven; let cool.

You may substitute apple liquid instead of water to prepare glaze according to package directions. Spoon glaze over Apple Cheesecake, covering the apples well. You will only use half of the prepared glaze. Store the rest in a jar with a tight lid in the refrigerator for your next Apple Cheesecake. Glaze will keep for three weeks. Do not freeze.

* packaged

Apple Walnut Crisp

Filling:
2 cans (21 ounces each) prepared apple pie filling
1/2 cup white raisins
1/4 cup currants
1/4 cup brown sugar, firmly packed
juice of 1 medium lemon
Topping:
4 ounces soft butter
1 egg, well beaten
1 teaspoon vanilla
1 cup all-purpose flour
1/2 cup walnuts, coarsely ground
1/2 teaspoon cinnamon
vanilla ice cream or whipped cream (optional)

Filling: Mix apple pie filling with raisins, brown sugar and lemon juice. Turn into an ungreased 9x13-inch baking dish. Cover; keep at room temperature.

Topping: Work butter, egg, vanilla, flour, walnuts and cinnamon with fingertips until all ingredients are blended. Crumble evenly over apple mixture.

Bake at 350 degrees for 25 minutes or until topping is golden brown and apple mixture is bubbling. Remove from oven. Serve warm with ice cream or whipped cream.

Serves 6 to 8

Berry Cobbler
with Ginger Whipped Cream

Filling:
4 cups fresh or frozen (defrosted) blueberries
2 tablespoons lemon juice
4 tablespoons brown sugar
2 tablespoons *Wondra* flour
Topping:
4 ounces butter, softened
1 cup flour
1/3 cup sugar
1/2 teaspoon cinnamon
1 teaspoon vanilla
Ginger Whipped Cream:
1/2 pint whipped cream, well chilled
1 tablespoon powdered sugar
2 tablespoons minced crystallized ginger
1 tablespoon Courvoisier

   Combine topping ingredients; work with fingertips until coarse.
   To assemble, place blueberries into 9-inch baking dish; add lemon juice and sugar. Sprinkle with flour. Crumble topping over berries. Bake at 350 degrees for 35 minutes or until golden brown and berry mixture bubbles.
   Before whipping cream, chill bowl and beaters in freezer. Whip cream; fold in sugar, ginger and Courvoisier. Chill.
   Serve cobbler warm with ginger whipped cream.
   Serves 6 to 8

Black Forest Trifle

1 package any dark chocolate cake mix
2 packages custard
2 (17-ounce) cans bing cherries, well drained
1 pint heavy cream
2 tablespoons powdered sugar
1/4 cup dry sherry
1/2 cup dark chocolate shavings

Prepare chocolate cake according to package directions. Bake in two 9-inch cake pans.

Prepare custard according to package directions. Pour into 2 shallow bowls; cover and chill.

Assemble about 2 hours before your guests arrive.

Whip cream with powdered sugar.

In trifle bowl, place the first layer of chocolate cake*, sprinkle with half of the sherry, followed by one bowl of custard, half of the cherries, and half of the whipped cream. Repeat layers. Top with chocolate shavings. Chill.

Serves 8 to 10

*You may have to trim the chocolate cake layers to fit your trifle bowl.

Blueberry Hazelnut Crumble

Filling:
6 cups fresh or frozen blueberries
1/2 cup brown sugar, firmly packed
1/4 cup sugar
juice of 1 medium lemon
4 tablespoons *Wondra* flour
Topping:
4 ounces soft butter
1 egg, well beaten
1 teaspoon vanilla
1 cup all-purpose flour
1/2 cup roasted hazelnuts, coarsely ground
vanilla ice cream or prepared whipped cream (optional)

Filling: Place blueberries in ungreased 9x12-inch baking dish. Add brown sugar and lemon juice. Sprinkle evenly with flour.

Topping: Work butter, egg, vanilla, flour and hazelnuts with fingertips until all ingredients are blended. Crumble evenly over blueberry mixture.

Bake at 375 degrees for 25 minutes.

Serve warm (with ice cream or whipped cream if desired).

Serves 8 to 12

Death by Chocolate Mousse Cake

Filling:
1 package *(Alsa* or any brand) chocolate mousse
Cake:
4 ounces bittersweet chocolate
1 teaspoon vanilla
1 tablespoon espresso, brewed
6 tablespoons butter
1/2 cup sugar
2 tablespoon Courvoisier
3 eggs, separated
1/2 cup ground almonds

Prepare mousse according to instructions on package; substitute half and half for milk, add 1 tablespoon Courvoisier.

Combine chocolate, vanilla, espresso, butter, sugar and brandy in a saucepan. Heat until butter is melted. Remove pan from heat; let cool down.

Beat egg yolks until lemon-colored; stir into chocolate mixture. Whip egg whites until stiff; fold into chocolate mixture.

Turn batter into 8-inch buttered springform pan.

Bake at 300 degrees (in middle of oven) for 45 minutes. Cool completely on a rack and remove sides of pan.

Cut chocolate cake in half horizontally (carefully!). Place layer on serving platter or cake stand, fill evenly with half of chocolate mousse; top with second half of cake. Use remaining mousse like icing. Sprinkle with almonds. Chill for at least 4 hours before serving.

Serves 6 to 8

Debbie's Lemon Baba

This is the kind of project you undertake when nothing else needs your attention and your Aunt Millie from Philly is coming to visit for a week. A lot of work but worth it!

Baba:
1 tablespoon melted butter (to coat pan)
powdered sugar
2 to 3 lemons
1/2 cup plus 3/4 cup granulated sugar, divided
3/4 cup whole milk
4 ounces butter or margarine
2/3 cup cake flour
6 large eggs, separated
dash salt
Sauce:
1 cup sour cream
2 tablespoons heavy cream
1/2 cup sugar
3 to 4 tablespoons fresh lemon juice

Baba: Brush 12-cup bundt pan with melted butter. Sprinkle with powdered sugar and shake out excess; set aside.

Peel the skins off 2 small lemons, cutting off all the white pith. Squeeze the lemons to make 1/3 cup juice. Place peel in food processor with a metal blade, add 1/2 cup sugar and juice and process until peel is minced as finely as the sugar (about 1 minute).

Transfer lemon mixture to an 8-cup microwaveable measuring cup. Add milk and butter; microwave, covered, on high for 2 to 3 minutes. Return to food processor; add flour and process for 20 seconds to combine. With machine running, add egg yolks and process for 20 seconds. Pour in lemon juice and process.

In a large mixing bowl, beat egg whites and a pinch of salt with an electric mixer until soft peaks form. Beating continuously, mix in 3/4 cup sugar (2 tablespoons at a time) until stiff (but not dry) peaks form. Partially fold a third of the yolk mixture into whites, then fold in the remainder. Spoon into prepared bundt pan, spreading top evenly.

Place pan in 3-inch-deep baking pan filled with 1 to 2 inches of hot water in center of 325-degree oven. Bake for 50 to 55 minutes, or until top is golden and cracked. Transfer to a cooling rack for 15 minutes; invert onto a platter.

Sauce: Stir together; refrigerate. Spoon small amount of sauce onto dessert plate. Top with (microwaved) warm cake. Garnish with thinly sliced lemon and a sprig of mint.

Enjoy! Unless you're worn out from all this work.

Serves 6 to 8

Last-Minute Summer Trifle

1 *(Sara Lee)* pound cake, thickly sliced
2 packages custard mix (follow instructions)
2 tablespoons dry sherry or Cointreau
1 pint heavy cream, whipped*
1 tablespoon powdered sugar
3 cups strawberries, cleaned and cut in half
2 cups blueberries
(reserve a few of each berry for garnish)

Prepare custard the day before according to directions on package. Pour custard into two shallow bowls; refrigerate.

Whip cream with powdered sugar.

In a trifle bowl, place a layer of sliced pound cake; add half of mixed berries. Drizzle with 1 tablespoon sherry; then add half of custard. Distribute evenly. Add half of whipped cream. Repeat layers, ending with whipped cream; garnish — refrigerate.

Layers of fresh fruit can be changed to well-drained canned fruit of your choice.

Serves 8

*Always chill bowl and beaters before whipping cream.

Lemon Cheesecake

Crust:
6 tablespoons butter
2 tablespoons brown sugar
1 cup graham cracker crumbs
Filling:
16 ounces cream cheese (room temperature)
1/2 cup sugar
zest of 1 lemon
juice of 2 lemons
1 whole egg
1/2 teaspoon vanilla
Topping:
4 ounces sour cream
2 tablespoons sugar

Preheat oven to 375 degrees. In a heavy skillet, melt butter. Add brown sugar; dissolve over medium heat. Remove from heat; add graham cracker crumbs and blend well. Pat mixture firmly into a 9- or 10-inch springform. Do not build up sides.

In a bowl, beat cream cheese and sugar with electric mixer on medium. Add zest of lemon and lemon juice. Beat in egg slowly; add vanilla. Pour filling into springform.

In a separate bowl, beat sour cream and sugar until well blended. Drizzle over cheese filling.

Place on foil-lined cookie sheet. Bake for 15 minutes. Remove, cool, and freeze.

Serve semi-frozen. Top with fresh berries or raspberry sauce. Delicious! Refreeze leftovers.

Serves 8 to 10

Lemon Mousse
(with Ladyfingers)

3 lemons
4 eggs, separated
1/2 cup plus 1 tablespoon granulated sugar
1 tablespoon gelatin
1 pint whipping cream, whipped
1 tablespoon powdered sugar
18 ladyfingers*
toasted slivered almonds (optional)

Grate rind of two lemons; reserve. Squeeze juice from all three lemons; reserve.

Combine egg yolks with rind and 1/2 cup sugar; beat until mixture is lemon-colored. Place in double boiler; heat through, stirring occasionally.

Combine lemon juice and gelatin; microwave for 10 seconds to dissolve, add to egg mixture.

Whip cream until peaks form; add powdered sugar; reserve. Whip egg whites with 1 tablespoon sugar; reserve.

Remove egg and lemon mixture from double boiler; cool for 5 minutes. Gently fold in whipped cream; blend. Fold in egg whites; blend.

Line 6 parfait glasses with ladyfingers. Spoon lemon mousse into parfait glasses . You may also place ladyfingers against the sides of a glass serving bowl and bring to the table. Then dish out portions on plates. Chill at least 4 hours before serving.

Serves 6

*packaged

Night and Day Chocolate Mousse
on Hazelnut Meringues

4 egg whites
1 cups sugar
1 cup finely ground hazelnuts
3/4 teaspoon vanilla
1 package *(Alsa*)* white chocolate mousse mix
1 package *(Alsa*)* dark chocolate mousse mix

Meringues: In a bowl with electric mixer beat egg whites until whites hold peaks. Add sugar slowly, beating until meringue holds stiff, glossy peaks. Gently fold in ground nuts and vanilla. Drop by tablespoons onto parchment-covered cookie sheet. Spread to 2-inch circles. Bake at 250 degrees for 1 hour. Turn off oven and let meringues dry out. Store in airtight container.

Mousse: Prepare mousse mixes, each in its own bowl, according to package directions, except: substitute half and half for milk. Cover and chill for at least 2 hours.

To assemble: Place 1 meringue round on dessert dish; top with a 1-inch layer of white mousse. Top with a second meringue and finish with a layer of dark mousse. Garnish with 2 teaspoons of white mousse. You can also prepare this dessert in parfait glasses if you crumble the meringues. Either way, it's a delightful dessert.

Serves 6 to 8

*or any brand of mousse

Peach Cobbler

Filling:
3 cups sliced, drained, canned (or fresh) peaches (reserve
  syrup)
1 teaspoon grated lemon rind
2 teaspoons lemon juice
1/2 teaspoon almond extract
4 tablespoons brown sugar
2 tablespoons *Wondra* flour
Dough:
4 ounces soft butter
1 cup flour
1/2 cup plus 2 teaspoons sugar
1 teaspoon vanilla

Filling: Arrange peaches in a buttered 8-inch square
baking dish. Sprinkle with mixture of 1/4 cup peach syrup,
lemon rind, lemon juice, almond extract and sugar.
Sprinkle with flour. Heat in a preheated 400-degree oven
for about 5 minutes while preparing cobbler dough.

Dough: With fingertips work together butter, flour,
sugar and vanilla. Crumble dough over peach mixture and
sprinkle with 2 tablespoons sugar. Bake at 375 degrees for
30 minutes.

You may serve with a dollop of whipped cream or ice
cream.

Serves 6 to 8

Peach Walnut Crisp

Filling:
6 large fresh peaches, peeled and sliced
1/2 cup brown sugar, firmly packed
juice of 1 medium lemon
3 tablespoons *Wondra* flour
Topping:
4 ounces soft butter
1 teaspoon vanilla
1/2 cup walnuts, coarsely ground
1 cup all-purpose flour
vanilla ice cream or whipped cream (optional)

Filling: Place sliced peaches in ungreased 9x12-inch baking dish. Add brown sugar and lemon juice. Sprinkle evenly with *Wondra* flour.

Topping: Work butter, vanilla, walnuts and flour with fingertips until all ingredients are blended. Crumble evenly over peach mixture.

Bake at 375 degrees for 25 minutes, or until topping is golden brown and filling bubbles.

Serves 6 to 8

Silesian Walnut Pastry Crescents

Dough:
1 cup flour
1 cup small curd dry cottage cheese
4 ounces butter, softened
Filling:
1-1/2 cups walnuts, finely ground
1 egg white
3 tablespoons powdered sugar

Combine all ingredients for dough. Work with finger-tips; form into ball. Wrap and refrigerate for one hour.

Combine all ingredients for filling.

Roll out dough to 1/8-inch thickness. Cut into 5-inch squares. Cut across squares to form two triangles. Place 2 tablespoons of filling on long end of triangle. Roll up tightly, seal, and form into crescent; pinch ends of crescent to seal.

Bake at 350 degrees for 15 to 20 minutes.

Place in airtight containers or freeze.

Makes about 24 crescents

Strawberry Fool

2 pints fresh strawberries
1 cup fresh strawberries, sliced
3 tablespoons Cointreau
1 pint heavy cream
2 tablespoons powdered sugar

Purée 2 pints of strawberries with 2 tablespoons Cointreau in food processor. Push through a sieve to remove seeds. Chill.

Whip cream; add powdered sugar, 1 tablespoon Cointreau. Fold into berry purée.

In stemmed glass, layer sliced strawberries, followed by whipped cream mixture. Repeat layers, ending with cream. Top with a ripe strawberry.

Serves 6

Viennese Nut Torte

6 ounces unsalted butter, softened
3/4 cup sugar
1 pound shelled walnuts, chopped medium-fine in food
    processor
3 tablespoons instant espresso, dissolved in 1/2 cup hot
    water
1/2 cup half and half
1 (12-ounce) package vanilla wafers
1/2 pint whipping cream
2 tablespoons powdered sugar

In a bowl, beat butter and sugar by hand until creamy.
Add walnuts; blend. Add half of hot coffee mixture; blend.
    In a shallow bowl, pour half and half; add rest of
coffee. Dip vanilla wafers into coffee mixture (quickly —
in and out). Layer bottom of 9-inch springform pan with
wafers. Fill in bare spots with wafer crumbs. Top with half
of nut mixture; repeat, ending with wafer layer. Wrap in
plastic; freeze (for as long as four months).
    Before serving, whip cream with powdered sugar.
Release springform rim; place torte on serving platter. Use
whipped cream like any icing and cover top and sides
evenly; decorate with walnut halves. Return to freezer for
about one hour to firm topping; serve frozen. Offer small
portions — it's rich! Cover leftover torte tightly with
plastic wrap and return to freezer till the next party.

Serves 12

Beef, Lamb and Pork

Basic Marinara Sauce

2 tablespoons olive oil

1 medium onion, finely chopped

3 cloves garlic, finely chopped (or 1 teaspoon prepared
    crushed garlic)

2 (14-1/2 -ounce) cans crushed Italian tomatoes

3 (14-1/2 -ounce) cans Italian tomatoes

1 tablespoon fresh basil (or 2 teaspoons dried)

1 teaspoon dried oregano

1-1/4 teaspoons sugar (or 1 package sugar substitute)

2 teaspoons Italian seasoning

    In a heavy 4-quart saucepan or dutch oven, heat oil;
sauté onion and garlic for 5 minutes. Add all other ingredients. Simmer on low for at least 2 hours.

    This is the basic sauce I use for all dishes that require
a tomato sauce: Lasagna, Meatball Linguine, Stuffed
Crêpes, etc.

    I keep at least two quarts of Marinara in the freezer:
Be prepared!

    Note: If sauce gets too thick, add nonfat, low salt
chicken broth to suit.

    You may double this recipe.

    Makes about 3 quarts

Beef Stroganoff

4 ounces butter or margarine
1 large onion, minced
2-1/2-pound round steak (have butcher cut in 2-inch
    strips), dredged in 1/4 cup flour
1 pound mushrooms, sliced
1 cup beef broth (fat free)
8 ounces sour cream
3 tablespoons worcestershire sauce
1/2 cup catsup
salt and pepper to taste
egg noodle or rice

Heat butter in heavy Dutch oven or electric skillet on high. Sauté onion for 3 minutes. Add flour-coated meat in batches; brown on all sides. Add mushrooms and beef broth.

Reduce heat and simmer for one hour or until meat is tender. Store at this point or continue.

Combine sour cream, worcestershire and catsup. Pour over meat mixture, blending quickly; heat through. Remove from heat.

Serve over egg noodles, or rice.

Serves 6 to 8

Ham and Noodle Casserole

1 pound wide egg noodles
1 pound cooked or baked ham, diced
12 ounces sharp cheddar cheese, shredded
3 tablespoons butter
1/2 cup parmesan cheese, freshly grated

Boil noodles in 4 quarts of water until *al dente,* about 8 minutes; drain.

Butter the bottom of 9 x13-inch baking dish. Place half of noodles in dish; add half of ham and cheddar; dot with half of butter. Repeat with remaining noodles, ham and cheddar and butter.

At this point, you can refrigerate it for as long as three days, or freeze it.

If refrigerated or frozen, let dish come to room temperature before placing in oven.

Preheat oven to 350 degrees. Sprinkle casserole with parmesan, cover with foil, and bake for 25 minutes. Uncover and bake for 10 more minutes. Let it rest for 10 minutes and serve.

Serve with extra parmesan (optional).

Serves 6 to 8

Lasagna Bolognese

2 tablespoons olive oil
4 cloves garlic, chopped fine
1 medium onion, chopped fine
1/2 pound mushrooms, sliced
1-1/2 pounds extra-lean ground beef
3 cups Basic Marinara Sauce (see recipe)
2 cups canned stewed tomato pieces with juice
1 teaspoon spaghetti sauce seasoning
1/8 teaspoon cayenne pepper
2 tablespoons fresh basil or 1 teaspoon dried basil
1 teaspoon sugar
16 ounces mozzarella cheese, shredded
1 cup parmesan cheese, freshly grated
8 ounces ricotta or low-fat cottage cheese
12 ounces no-boil lasagna noodles

In a large dutch oven, sauté garlic, onion and mushrooms in olive oil on medium for about 5 minutes. Add ground beef; cook thoroughly. Add marinara sauce, stewed tomatoes, seasonings and sugar; slow-simmer for one hour.

In the bottom of a 9 x13-inch baking dish, pour a thin layer of meat sauce. Arrange a layer of pasta on top, pour on more sauce, and add one-third of each of the cheeses. Layer pasta, meat sauce and cheeses for two more layers. Top with parmesan cheese.

Can be stored for three days or frozen at this point.

Preheat oven to 350 degrees. Place lasagna on foil-covered cookie sheet; cover lightly with foil. Bake for 25 minutes; remove foil cover and bake until cheese is melted and sauce bubbles, about 15 minutes more. Form foil tent and let settle for 10 to 15 minutes before serving. Garnish with fresh basil leaves. Offer additional parmesan cheese (about 1 cup).

Serves 8 and more

Leg of Lamb
(with Moroccan Sauce)

1 leg of lamb
1 quart buttermilk
2 cloves garlic, thickly sliced
4 slices bacon
1/2 cup water
1/2 cup burgundy (or any dry red wine)
salt and pepper to taste

Lamb: Place lamb in Dutch oven, add buttermilk, cover and refrigerate for 24 hours. Turn at least twice.

Remove leg of lamb from marinade. Rinse with luke warm water and pat dry. With a sharp knife make eight slits in meat and stuff with garlic bits. Drape bacon slices over leg of lamb. Place on rack in roasting pan (with water covering bottom). Insert meat thermometer in meaty part of leg, or use instant meat thermometer.

Place in 350-degree oven; bake uncovered until meat thermometer registers medium rare or desired temperature (20 minutes per pound). Baste with wine several times while baking.

Remove from oven and let rest for 10 minutes before slicing.

Moroccan Sauce

2 tablespoons butter
1 shallot, finely chopped
6 dried apricot halves, finely chopped
3 dried prunes, finely chopped
2 dried peach halves, finely chopped
2 tablespoon currants
1/2 cup chicken broth
2 tablespoons teriyaki sauce
2 tablespoons tomato paste or puree
1/2 teaspoon dried rosemary
1/4 teaspoon black pepper
2 tablespoons brandy

Melt butter; sauté shallot for 2 minutes over medium heat. Add dried fruit, saute for 5 minutes. Add chicken broth and all other ingredients except brandy; simmer slowly for 10 minutes. Cook down to half the amount of liquid.

Add brandy and simmer 5 minutes. Store or serve.

Serve sauce separately (in gravy boat) for guests to help themselves.

Meatballs Marinara

1 pound extra-lean ground beef
1 medium onion, finely chopped
1 tablespoon worcestershire sauce
1 tablespoon Dijon mustard
1/4 cup Italian breadcrumbs
1/2 teaspoon garlic powder
1/4 teaspoon oregano
1/2 teaspoon basil
1 egg
salt and pepper to taste
4 tablespoons olive oil
1 clove garlic, minced
1 pound Italian (chicken) sausage, sliced to 1/4-inch
    thickness
8 cups basic marinara sauce (see recipe)

Place first 10 ingredients into a large bowl. Work with your fingers until mixture is well blended. Form meatballs from about 2 generous tablespoons of meat (or desired size).

In a heavy skillet, heat oil with garlic. In batches, quickly brown meatballs. Remove from skillet onto paper towels. Lightly brown sausage in same skillet. Drain on paper towels.

In a large dutch oven, slowly heat marinara sauce (see basic recipe); add meatballs and sausage. Cover and simmer on low heat for 1 hour.

Can be prepared several days ahead; refrigerate (or freeze for use later). You'll have it for emergencies! Before reheating, let come to room temperature.

Serve with 1-1/2 pounds of your choice of pasta;
follow cooking directions.
Serves 8 to 12

You can divide this sauce with meatballs and Italian
sausage into 2 equal batches. Each will serve 4 to 6.

Shepherd's Pie

6 tablespoons margarine
2 cloves garlic, chopped
1 large onion, chopped
8 ounces mushrooms, sliced
2 pounds lean beef stew, cubed, fat trimmed
1 can beef broth (low sodium, fat free, if available)
2 large tomatoes, peeled and diced
1 cup Pinot Noir or any other dry red wine
2 tablespoons Dijon mustard
2 tablespoons worcestershire sauce
salt and pepper to taste
1 (8-ounce) can sliced carrots, drained
1 cup frozen green peas
1 (8-ounce) can small onions, drained
3 cups mashed potatoes (when using instant mashed
    potatoes, follow directions)
1 egg

In a heavy Dutch oven, heat 2 tablespoons margarine. Add garlic, onions and mushrooms; sauté for about 6 minutes. Remove to paper towel and set aside.

Heat remaining margarine; add beef and quickly brown on all sides on high Add broth, tomatoes, wine, mustard, worcestershire; salt and pepper to taste, turn down heat.

Simmer on low for 2 hours. Let come to room temperature. Refrigerate or freeze at this point. Can be prepared three days ahead or frozen at this point.

Before serving: Add reserved onion and mushroom mixture, carrots, frozen peas, and onions. Place all in 4-quart round, oval or square casserole or baking dish.

Prepare mashed potatoes according to directions, or use your favorite mashed potato recipe (including garlic mashed potatoes). Store or freeze at this point. Can be prepared three days in advance.

Before baking, let come to room temperature. Beat the egg and blend into mashed potatoes.

Circle mashed potato mixture around sides of casserole to form a wreath; try not to let potatoes touch sides. If there is not enough liquid in the meat mixture, add chicken broth and a dash of red wine. Bake at 350 degrees for 30 minutes, or until thoroughly heated and potato ring turns golden.

Serves 6 to 8

Veal Marsala

3 tablespoons olive oil
2 cloves garlic, minced
2 large shallots, finely chopped
3 tablespoons butter
2-1/2 pounds veal scallops
1/2 cup flour
1 pound mushrooms, sliced
1/2 cup marsala
1 (14-1/2 -ounce) can stewed, sliced Italian tomatoes
salt and pepper to taste

Heat oil on medium-high; sauté garlic and shallots for 3 minutes. Push to edges of skillet. Add butter; gently toss veal with flour in a plastic or paper bag. Shake off excess flour and brown flour-drenched veal in batches for 2 minutes on each side. (You may have to add 1 or 2 more tablespoons olive oil.)

Remove from skillet and set aside. Sauté mushrooms for 5 minutes; return veal to skillet. Add marsala and tomatoes. Let come to a soft boil. Remove from heat; let stand at room temperature until ready to serve.

Reheat slowly — do not let food stick to bottom of skillet. Do not overcook veal — it can turn tough.

Serves 8

Meatless Meals

Crêpes
(with Mushroom-Spinach, Beef, or Chicken Filling)

Basic Crêpes:
3 eggs
11/2 cups flour
11/2 cups plus 6 tablespoons milk
6 tablespoons butter or margarine

Whisk eggs and flour together; add milk.

In a large, heavy skillet (15 to 17 inches diameter), over medium heat melt 1 teaspoon butter. With a small ladle, pour enough batter into skillet to evenly and thinly cover most of the pan. (Tilt skillet to distribute batter.)

After 3 minutes, gently loosen crêpe and quickly flip; cook second side for just a blink! Remove crêpe to platter. Repeat until all batter has been used.

Stack crêpes; cover and refrigerate (as long as three days) until ready to use.

Mushroom-Spinach Filling:
10 ounces frozen spinach, defrosted and squeezed dry
2 tablespoons butter
1/2 pound fresh mushrooms, chopped
2 shallots, minced
1/2 cup cottage cheese
3 ounces fontina cheese, grated
1 egg

1/4 teaspoon nutmeg
salt and pepper to taste

Melt butter; sauté shallots and mushrooms over
medium heat in heavy skillet for 8 minutes. Add spinach
and nutmeg and simmer for 4 minutes gently stirring.
Remove skillet from heat. Let mixture cool a bit and turn
into a bowl. Fold in egg and cottage and fontina cheeses.
Place about 3 tablespoons of filling on the edge of each
crêpe, roll up tightly and place in buttered baking dish,
seam-side down. Top with Bêchamel-Caper Sauce.

Bêchamel-Caper Sauce:
4 tablespoons butter
1/4 cup flour
2 cups chicken stock
1 tablespoon lemon juice
1 tablespoon parsley
2 tablespoons capers
1/2 teaspoon sugar
salt and pepper to taste

Melt butter in heavy skillet; add flour. Gradually add
chicken broth, blending into flour-butter paste. Do not let
lumps form! When mixture reaches desired thickness, add
remaining ingredients. Bake at 350 degrees, covered for 15
minutes, and uncovered for 5 minutes.

Beef Filling:
2 tablespoons olive oil
1 large shallot, finely minced
1 clove garlic, minced

1 pound extra-lean ground beef
1 egg, beaten
1 teaspoon Dijon mustard
1 tablespoon Worcestershire sauce
4 ounces fontina cheese, shredded
1/2 cup parmesan cheese, grated
2 cups prepared marinara sauce
salt and pepper to taste

Heat oil in heavy skillet; sauté shallot and garlic for 3 minutes. Add meat; brown quickly, about 8 minutes while stirring constantly. Use fork to crumble meat into tiny bits. Remove meat mixture from skillet to a mixing bowl. Add egg, cheeses, salt and pepper. Blend well. Place 3 to 4 tablespoons meat filling near one end of each crêpe; roll tightly. Place seam-side down in lightly buttered baking dish. Top with marinara sauce and sprinkle with parmesan cheese.

Bake, covered with foil, at 350 degrees for 15 minutes. Remove foil and bake until sauce bubbles, about 10 minutes more. Serve with extra marinara sauce and parmesan cheese for individual helpings.

Chicken Filling:
2 whole skinless chicken breasts, cooked and diced small
2/3 cup tiny frozen green peas
2 tablespoons capers
2 tablespoons chopped artichokes hearts
1 tablespoon worcestershire sauce
Quick Hollandaise Sauce (see recipe)
salt and pepper to taste

Mix chicken cubes, peas, capers, artichokes, worcester-shire sauce with 1/2 of prepared hollandaise sauce. Place about 3 to 4 tablespoons chicken mixture onto each crêpe; roll tightly. Place seam-side down in lightly buttered baking dish. Top with remaining Hollandaise; cover with foil.

Bake in 350-degree oven for 15 minutes; uncover and bake 10 more minutes. Let rest 5 minutes. Serve.

Herbed Mushroom Rice

1 package prepared herbed rice
1(4-ounce) can mushrooms, drained

Prepare rice as directed*. Add mushrooms.
Serves 4 to 6

*For a better taste, substitute juice from mushrooms
and fat-free chicken broth for water. Excellent flavor!

Pasta Primavera

3 medium tomatoes, seeded, chopped
6 ounces brie cheese, cut into bits
3 tablespoons fresh basil, chopped
1/2 cup olive oil
1 cup pea pods, cut in half
3/4 cup tiny green peas, defrosted
1/2 cup broccoli flourets
1 (8-ounce) can mushrooms, well drained
1/4 cup water
1-1/2 pounds fresh linguine
1/4 cup cream
1 cup parmesan cheese, grated

Early in the morning: Place tomatoes, brie and basil in a storage container and add olive oil. Cover and toss. Let stand at room temperature for as long as 8 hours. Toss occasionally.

Place all vegetables with 1/4 cup water in microwave-safe container, cook for 3 minutes. Drain and let stand at room temperature, covered, till ready to use.

Just before serving: In a large pot, bring 6 quarts water to a rolling boil; add linguine. Let boil for no more than 4 minutes. Drain in colander and immediately return to still-warm pot. Add vegetables and oil/brie/tomato/basil mixture. Toss gently and add cream.

Serve with a sprinkling of parmesan, or let your guests help themselves to the amount of cheese they want.

Serves 6 to 8

Rice and Gnocchi

1 package prepared rice
low-fat chicken broth

I use all kinds of prepared rice and follow instructions, except I substitute low-fat chicken broth for the water.

Gnocchi comes straight from that little old gnocchi-maker. (Can be purchased frozen at grocery store, or fresh from an Italian deli.) Prepare according to instructions. Great!

Vegetarian Lasagna

1/4 cup olive oil
1 large onion, finely chopped
3 cloves garlic, finely chopped (or 1 teaspoon prepared
    crushed garlic)
1 green zucchini, sliced medium-fine
1 yellow zucchini, sliced medium-fine
1 pound fresh mushrooms, sliced
1 red bell pepper, cut into fine strips
12 (no-cook) lasagna noodles
4 cups Basic Marinara Sauce (see recipe)
8 ounces low-fat ricotta cheese
16 ounces mozzarella cheese
1 cup parmesan cheese, grated

In a heavy Dutch oven, heat oil; sauté onion and garlic
for 3 minutes. Add remaining vegetables in batches and
sauté about 4 minutes each batch. Remove to paper towels.

In a 9 x13-inch glass baking dish, pour about 1 cup of
marinara, layer 6 lasagna noodles, half of vegetables, half
of ricotta, one-third of mozzarella, and 1 cup marinara.
Sprinkle with parmesan cheese. Repeat layers, ending with
parmesan. Refrigerate or freeze at this point. Allow to
lasagna reach room temperature before baking.

Preheat oven to 350 degrees. Place lasagna on foil-
covered cookie sheet; cover lightly with foil. Bake for 25
minutes; remove foil and bake until cheese is melted and
sauce bubbles, about 15 minutes more. Let settle for 10 to
15 minutes before serving. Garnish with fresh basil leaves.
Offer additional parmesan cheese (about 1 cup).

Serves 8 and more

Poultry

Chicken Paprikash

1/4 cup flour
6 to 8 chicken breast halves (boneless, skin on)
4 ounces butter or margarine
1 medium onion, chopped
2 tablespoons paprika
1 teaspoon sugar
1 pound mushrooms, sliced
1 can consommé
salt and pepper to taste
1 cup sour cream (do not use fat-free sour cream)

Place flour in plastic bag. Dredge chicken pieces in flour until evenly coated, shake off excess flour. Heat butter in large electric skillet or dutch oven. Add onions; sauté 3 minutes. Add paprika and sugar.

Place chicken in skillet, skin-side down, and brown slightly for 5 minutes. Turn and brown other side. Turn skin side up and add mushrooms. Pour consommé over meat. Cover; simmer for 15 minutes.

Store until ready to serve. Can be prepared one day ahead. Before serving, reheat; remove breasts to platter. Blend sour cream into liquid; return chicken to skillet. Cover and reheat for 1 minute. Serve.

Note: You can "hold" serving this meal without ruining it. Tastes great anytime! Always reheat slowly.

Serves 6 to 8

Cold Sliced Lemon/Teriyaki Chicken Breasts
for Summer Buffet

2 tablespoons butter
6 to 8 chicken breasts (boneless, skin on)
1/4 cup lemon juice and 1 lemon, sliced
1/4 cup teriyaki cooking sauce/marinade
1 tablespoon orange zest

Place chicken breasts in lightly buttered baking dish, skin-side up. Combine lemon juice, teriyaki sauce, and orange zest; pour over chicken. Let stand for 4 to 6 hours, turning chicken pieces a few times.

Bake, covered, at 350 degrees for 20 minutes. Uncover and bake an additional 15 minutes at 375 degrees.

Remove from baking dish. Chill; slice* before serving. Arrange on platter among greens and lemon slices.

Serves 6 to 8

*Discard skin before slicing. Baking the chicken with the skin on keeps the meat moist and adds flavor.

Honey Chicken Surprise

6 to 8 chicken breasts
1/2 cup Italian dressing
6 ounces pineapple jam
6 ounces apricot jam
2 tablespoons lemon juice
2 tablespoons honey
2 tablespoons worcestershire sauce
1 teaspoon Dijon mustard
1 package dry onion soup
salt and pepper to taste

The day before: Place chicken in baking dish, skin-side up. Marinate chicken in Italian dressing; cover and refrigerate.

In a 1-quart saucepan, slowly heat jams, lemon juice, honey, worcestershire, mustard, and onion soup. Remove from heat; store at room temperature.

The next day: Drain half of marinade from chicken, add jam mixture; cover. Keep at room temperature until ready to cook.

Cover chicken with foil. Preheat oven to 400 degrees. Bake 20 minutes covered. Lower heat to 350 degrees, uncover, and bake an additional 15 minutes.

Serves 6 to 8

Lemon Chicken Florentine

2 tablespoons butter
1 medium onion, finely chopped
1 clove garlic, finely minced
2 (8-ounce) packages frozen spinach, defrosted and
    squeezed dry
1/2 teaspoon nutmeg
1/2 teaspoon paprika
salt and pepper to taste
1 tablespoon butter or margarine
6 to 8 chicken breast halves
juice of 2 lemons
1/4 cup dry white wine
1/2 teaspoon rosemary
roasted red pepper strips

One day ahead: Sauté onion and garlic in butter; add
spinach and spices. Blend. Cover and refrigerate.

In early afternoon: Place chicken in a lightly buttered
baking dish; pour lemon juice and wine over chicken.
Sprinkle with rosemary; cover. Keep at room temperature
until ready to bake.

Place chicken in preheated 350-degree oven. Cover,
bake for 30 minutes; uncover, bake till golden (about 15
minutes).

To serve: Reheat spinach mixture in microwave for 4
minutes on high. Place spinach (2 generous tablespoons) on
each dinner plate; pat flat (about the size of the chicken
portion); top with a piece of chicken. Spoon 2 tablespoons of
pan juice over chicken. Garnish with roasted pepper strips.

Serves 6 to 8

Mediterranean Chicken

4 tablespoons olive oil
2 tablespoons butter or margarine
1 medium onion, finely chopped
3 cloves garlic, finely chopped
6 to 8 chicken breast halves
1/4 cup flour
4 ounces black olives, sliced
1 pound mushrooms, sliced
2 (14-1/2 -ounce) cans sliced stewed Italian tomatoes
1/3 cup Marsala
1/2 cup *V-8 Juice*
salt and pepper to taste

In dutch oven or large electric skillet, sauté onion and garlic in oil/butter for 4 minutes; push to sides of skillet. Dredge chicken breasts in flour then brown quickly on both sides (golden brown) on medium high.

Add remaining ingredients; quickly bring to boil (do not cover — allow liquids to cook down a bit). Reduce heat; cover and simmer for 10 minutes. Remove from heat and let cool.

Cover and store in refrigerator; will keep for three days.

Before serving: Bring to room temperature; reheat slowly. Gently lift chicken pieces occasionally to prevent sticking to bottom of pan.

Serve, spooning several tablespoons of pan juice with mushrooms over each chicken portion. If served with gnocchi (pasta), cook pasta according to directions.

Serves 6 to 8

Roasted Cornish Game Hens
(with Rob's Wild Rice Cranberry Almond Stuffing)

1 teaspoon thyme
1 teaspoon Provençale seasoning
1 teaspoon salt
1/2 teaspoon pepper
4 game hens
2 strips bacon, cut in half

Blend herbs and spices. Rub birds, including cavities, with seasoning mixture.

Stuff birds with Rob's Wild Rice Cranberry Almond Dressing (see recipe); secure openings with small skewers. (I prefer to sew my birds shut — may be a holdover from my mother's sewing talents!) Fill bottom of roasting pan with 1 cup water. Place hens on rack in pan; place bacon half on each hen. Cover with foil, forming a tent.

Roast at 425 degrees for 20 minutes. Remove foil; reduce heat to 350 degrees. Roast for 30 more minutes, or until golden brown. Baste occasionally with pan drippings.

With poultry shears (or sharp knife), cut hens in half. Serve cut-side down.

Optional: garnish with greens and kumquats.

Serves 6 to 8

Rob's Wild Rice Cranberry Almond Dressing
for Game Hens

4 ounces wild rice (cook according to instructions)
2 cups chicken stock
2 ounces butter
1 medium onion, finely chopped
1/2 cup celery, finely chopped
1 cup raw whole cranberries
1/2 cup blanched almonds, coarsely chopped
1/2 teaspoon sage

Prepare wild rice (substitute chicken stock for water). Sauté onions and celery in butter in heavy skillet until tender. Add to rice; blend well.

Add cranberries, almonds and sage. Fill game hens' cavities with dressing; secure with small skewers (or "sew" them shut with needle and thread). May be prepared the day before dinner party.

You can double and triple this recipe for larger fowl — capons, roasting chickens, or turkeys.

Makes enough stuffing for 4 to 6 game hens.

Salads and Salad Dressings

Asparagus on Tossed Greens

1-1/2 pounds asparagus
1 head red leaf lettuce (or 4 ounces mixed greens)
1 head Belgian endive
1 roasted red pepper, cut into strips

Break off asparagus stems (about one-third to one-half of total stem).

Cook asparagus in 1 cup water for 1 minute. Drain at once and cover with ice cubes to chill asparagus thoroughly. Wrap in paper towels; place in plastic bag. Refrigerate.

Before serving, toss greens with vinaigrette of your choice and divide evenly onto (chilled) salad plates. Divide asparagus stalks evenly on each serving and drape one or two strips of roasted red pepper crosswise over asparagus. Drizzle with 1 teaspoon dressing; serve.

Serves 6 to 8

Cæsar Salad

1 egg yolk
1 teaspoon anchovy paste
1 tablespoon Dijon mustard
2 teaspoons worcestershire sauce
1/4 cup olive oil
1 tablespoon mayonnaise (optional)
3 tablespoons fresh lemon juice
3 tablespoons red wine vinegar
1/3 cup parmesan cheese, freshly grated
1/4 teaspoon freshly ground black pepper

Blend all ingredients until smooth. Dressing keeps, covered and chilled, for two weeks.

Rinse Romaine lettuce, discard tough greens, tear into bite-size pieces. Spin dry.

Use only enough dressing to lightly coat salad greens. Do not overload!

Makes about 2 cups.

Chardonnay Vinaigrette

1 bottle *Lawry's* White Wine Vinaigrette
2 teaspoons sugar (or 2 packages sugar substitute)
1 teaspoon prepared horseradish
1 teaspoon Chardonnay

Discard 2 tablespoons oil from dressing. (Pour slowly as not to disturb dressing ingredients.) Add sugar, horseradish and Chardonnay to bottle. Shake well.

Allow to reach room temperature before serving.

Cider Vinaigrette

1 shallot, minced
1 tablespoon apple cider
2 tablespoons apple-cider vinegar
1/4 cup walnut oil
salt and freshly ground pepper
1 teaspoon sugar (or 1 pack sugar substitute)

In a small bowl, whisk together shallot, cider, and vinegar. Whisk in the walnut oil, and sugar, then season to taste with salt and pepper.

The cider and cider vinegar add an unusual and unexpected tang to this vinaigrette.

Keep at room temperature before using.

Cucumbers Emilié

4 cucumbers (or 2 English cucumbers)
1 teaspoon salt
1/4 cup white vinegar
2 tablespoons sugar
1/2 teaspoon black pepper

Peel cucumbers; slice paper-thin.* Place in bowl and toss with salt.

Refrigerate for 2 to 3 hours. Squeeze dry between folds of clean linen towel or strong paper towel..

Mix vinegar, sugar and pepper. Return cucumber to bowl; drizzle vinegar mixture over cucumbers. Cover tightly; refrigerate.

Serve on cup-like lettuce leaves. Can be prepared one day ahead.

Serves 6 to 8

*Slicing blade on four-sided shredder grater works well for slicing cucumbers thin.

Fruit Salad Medley
with Lemonade Dressing

2 oranges
2 apples
1 cup pineapple chunks (fresh or canned)
1 cup seedless grapes, halved
1 cup cantaloupe, diced
2 kiwi fruit, peeled and sliced
3 tablespoons Cointreau or other orange flavor liqueur

Lemonade Dressing:
juice of 2 large lemons
2 tablespoons sugar (or sugar substitute)
1/4 cup orange juice

Cut fruit into small chunks. Toss with orange liqueur and let sit for one hour.

Blend all dressing ingredients; shake well. (Dressing can be made 2 days ahead.) Place fruit in serving bowl; toss gently with dressing. Chill.

Serves 6 to 8

Garden Potato Salad

5 pounds red potatoes
1 Granny Smith apple, cored and finely diced
1 medium cucumber, peeled, seeded and finely diced
1 large red onion, finely chopped
4 tablespoons sweet cucumber relish, drained
1 teaspoon sugar
1 cup mayonnaise
salt and pepper to taste

Boil potatoes in skin about 20 minutes; do not overcook (must be firm). Cool. Peel and finely dice.

Combine all ingredients and toss with mayonnaise. Refrigerate. Prepare early in the day, cover and chill, for better flavor.

Garnish with touches of greens.

Green Peas and Water Chestnuts Salad

1 (10-ounce) package frozen tiny peas
1 (8-1/4-ounce) can sliced water chestnuts, well drained
1 (8-1/4-ounce) can sliced mushrooms, well drained
1 medium red onion, finely chopped
1/2 cup mayonnaise

Defrost peas; spread on paper towels and gently pat dry. In a large bowl, carefully toss all ingredients with mayonnaise.

Refrigerate for at least 4 hours before serving.

To prepare ahead: Omit mayonnaise until 1 hour before serving. Prepare as above.

Serves 6

Pickled Fresh Vegetable Relish

2 large, ripe tomatoes, peeled, seeded and chopped
1/2 cucumber, peeled, seeded, chopped, and squeezed dry
1/2 cup tiny frozen green peas, defrosted and patted dry
1/4 cup carrots, finely shredded
1/2 cup Chardonnay Vinaigrette (see recipe)
1 tablespoon balsamic vinegar

Place all vegetables in container. Add vinaigrette and balsamic vinegar.

Refrigerate. Shake occasionally. Keeps up to six days.

Prepare your choice of salad greens; toss with dressing of your choice. Sprinkle 3 tablespoons of vegetable relish over salad servings. Looks great — tastes great!

Serves 8 to 12 (salad portions)

Polka-Dot Vegetable Salad

1 medium-sized green zucchini, chopped fine
1 medium-sized yellow zucchini, chopped fine
1 green bell pepper, chopped fine
1 red bell pepper, chopped fine
1 English cucumber (if you use a regular cucumber,
    remove seeds), chopped fine
1 large red onion, chopped fine
2 cloves garlic, minced
1 small jalapeño pepper, seeded and minced (wear gloves
    for this chore)
6 large ripe tomatoes, seeded, chopped
3 dashes Tabasco
1/2 teaspoon ground pepper
2 tablespoons fresh cilantro, finely chopped
salt (optional)
4 tablespoons Chardonnay Vinaigrette (see recipe)
1 large avocado, diced
1/4 cup Chardonnay Vinaigrette

Day before: Combine all ingredients except avocado
and 1/4 cup Chardonnay Vinaigrette. Place in container,
cover tightly and refrigerate.

Before serving, add 1/4 cup more chardonnay vinaigrette. Serve on large red or green lettuce leaves.

Use diced avocado to garnish individual servings.
(Also: Without avocado added to vegetable mixture, salad
will keep fresh-tasting longer.)

Keeps for three days.

This salad takes time to prepare, but is worth the effort.

Serves 8

Raspberry Vinaigrette

1/4 cup raspberry vinegar
1/3 cup walnut oil
1/2 teaspoon cracked pepper
2 teaspoons sugar
1/2 teaspoon prepared horseradish

Blend all ingredients; shake well.
Keep at room temperature until ready to use.
Note: Top greens with 4 to 6 tablespoons roasted, crushed hazelnuts for variety.

Makes about 1/2 cup dressing.

Sliced Cucumbers
with Sour Cream-Chive Dressing

2 large cucumbers (English cucumbers preferably)
1 cup sour cream
4 tablespoons chives, chopped
2 teaspoons sugar (or 2 envelopes sugar substitute)
1/2 teaspoon cracked pepper
4 tablespoons tarragon vinegar
1/2 teaspoon dried tarragon
salt to taste

Slice cucumbers as thin as you can. Wrap in paper towels; place in container and chill for 4 hours.

Mix all other ingredients. Remove cucumbers from paper towels, place in bowl, and toss with sour cream dressing.

Serve on red lettuce or bibb lettuce leaves.

Looks great! Tastes great!

Serves 6 to 8

Spinach Salad with Dressing

2 bunches fresh spinach*
1/2 cup olive oil
3 tablespoons red wine vinegar
1 teaspoon crushed garlic
1/2 teaspoon oregano
1/8 teaspoon pepper
1 teaspoon sugar or 1 package sugar substitute
1 tablespoon parmesan cheese

Wash spinach thoroughly (in the morning); remove all stems and discard tough leaves. Spin dry; place in clean plastic bag and chill.

Combine all dressing ingredients, shake well and keep at room temperature.

Toss spinach with just enough dressing to coat all leaves.

Serves 6 to 8

* You may use "baby" spinach, it is a more tender leaf.

Spinach Salad
with Mandarin Slices

2 bunches fresh spinach
1 (4-1/2-ounce) can mandarin orange slices, drained
1/4 cup walnuts, chopped
vinaigrette of your choice

Wash spinach thoroughly (in the morning); remove all stems and discard tough leaves. Spin dry; place in clean plastic bag and chill.

With your favorite vinaigrette, toss spinach, mandarin orange slices and walnuts. Use just enough vinaigrette to evenly coat spinach — don't drown it!

Serves 6 to 8

Tomato Cucumber Salad
in Vinaigrette

1 large English or 2 regular cucumbers, peeled and sliced
    thin (squeezed dry)
6 medium tomatoes, peeled and sliced thin
1 small red onion, sliced thin
1/4 cup green onions, thinly sliced (green part only)
2 ounces Chardonnay Vinaigrette
2 tablespoons chopped fresh parsley
1 teaspoon sugar

In container or deep-rimmed platter, layer half of
cucumbers, tomatoes and green onions; repeat layers.
Sprinkle with half of Chardonnay Vinaigrette; cover and
refrigerate.

Place red onions in container with water and sugar;
refrigerate for several hours.

Three to four hours before serving: Remove onions
from water; pat dry. Scatter evenly over tomato-cucumber
mixture. Add rest of vinaigrette, cover and store until you
are ready to serve dinner.

Serve portions on large red leaf lettuce or Boston bibb
lettuce on chilled plates, or bring to the table on a serving
platter so your guests can help themselves. Either way,
sprinkle with parsley to garnish.

Serves 6 to 8

Tossed Greens

1 head red leaf lettuce, torn into pieces
4 cups wild greens *or* baby spinach, *all* stems removed
6 to 8 canned pear halves, drained
4 teaspoons pimiento, chopped
1 (8-ounce) bottle *Lawry's* White Wine Vinaigrette* (or
    any comparable dressing, except Italian)
2 teaspoons sugar substitute
1 tablespoon lemon juice

All greens must be rinsed and patted dry between pieces of paper towels so dressing can adhere. Toss greens with enough dressing to coat. Top with pear half, fill pear cavity with chopped pimiento, and serve.
Always shake well before serving.

Serves 6 to 8

* Prepare one bottle of *Lawry's* dressing: carefully discard about 2 tablespoons of oil from bottle; add sugar substitute and lemon juice; shake. Will keep at room temperature for several weeks.

Wild Greens

4 cups wild greens
1 head bibb lettuce, torn into bits
1 head Belgian endive
   or:
4 cups wild greens
1 head romaine lettuce, torn into bits
1 head Belgian endive
   or:
4 cups wild greens
1 head red leaf lettuce, torn into bits
1 head Belgian endive

Rinse greens; spin dry. Use dressing of choice and toss with greens. Divide into equal portions on salad plates and garnish each with your choice of:
   julienned fresh pears
   canned pear halves with pimento
   asparagus bundles
   vegetable relish

Serves 6 to 8

Salsas, Sauces and Condiments

Curried Fruit

1 (15-1/4-ounce) can pears, drained
1 (15-1/4-ounce) can peaches, drained
1 (15-1/4-ounce) can apricots, drained
2 (8-ounce) cans grapes, drained
3 tablespoons butter
1 teaspoon curry powder

Place fruit into an 8-inch baking dish. Melt butter with curry powder. Drizzle over fruit.

Bake uncovered in 350-degree oven for 15 minutes. Serve with chicken, turkey, or pork roast. Excellent!

Serves 6 to 8

Mango Salsa

2 ripe mangos, peeled and diced
1 yellow bell pepper, seeded and diced fine
1 large shallot, diced fine
2 tablespoons fresh lime juice
4 tablespoons green jalapeño jelly
2 tablespoons vegetable oil
1 tablespoon fresh cilantro, minced

Combine all ingredients in medium-sized bowl. Cover; refrigerate. May be made one day ahead.

Great for salmon, crab cakes, and lemon-roasted chicken.

Makes about 2 cups

Quick Hollandaise Sauce

4 tablespoons butter or margarine
1 package *Knorr* prepared Hollandaise Sauce (that's where
   the similarity ends!)
1 teaspoon sugar
1/2 cup milk
1/4 cup fat-free chicken broth
3 tablespoons lemon juice
1 egg yolk

   Melt butter; add package of Hollandaise and sugar,
blend. Reduce heat; slowly — in batches — add milk,
chicken broth, lemon juice; let come to soft boil stirring
constantly. Remove from heat. Let cool for 10 minutes.
Quickly beat in egg yolk.
   You can now store sauce. To serve later, reheat,
covered, in microwave.
   Optional: For caper lovers: Add 2 to 3 tablespoons
capers. (Someone once said: Everything that is good with
capers is good without capers!)

   Makes about 1 cup

Seafood

Bouillabaisse

Stock:
4 tablespoons olive oil
1 medium onion, finely chopped
3 cloves garlic
2 to 3 medium leeks (white to light green part only) finely
    chopped
1 fennel root, finely chopped
3 stalks celery, finely sliced
1 cup dry white wine
3 cups clam juice
2 cans sliced Italian tomatoes (14-1/2 ounces) with juice
dash pepper; salt optional
1/2 teaspoon thyme
1 bay leaf
1 pinch saffron
2 tablespoons chopped fresh parsley

2 ounces Pernod
24 large cooked, peeled deveined shrimp
1/2 pound rock shrimp
18 large scallops

Stock: Sauté onion, garlic, leeks, fennel root, and
celery for about 8 minutes. Add wine, clam juice,
tomatoes, pepper, thyme, bay leaf, saffron and parsley. Let
come to a quick boil; reduce heat and simmer for 3
minutes. Remove from heat.

At this point, stock can be refrigerated for up to five days.

Before serving: Reheat stock; add Pernod, shrimp, rock shrimp and scallops. Let come to a quick boil for 2 minutes. Remove from heat.

At the same time, steam clams.

Steamer clams:
1/2 cup dry white wine
2 tablespoons lemon juice
1 cup water
1 tablespoon butter
2 cloves garlic
32 to 40 clams

In separate 2-quart saucepan, heat wine, lemon juice, water, butter, garlic and clams. Boil until clams have opened up; discard broth and clams that remained closed.

Serve Bouillabaisse in soup bowls (not cups). Top each serving with 3 to 5 clams. Garnish with a sprig of fennel green.

This is a full meal and is simply elegant and delicious! Be ready to serve second helpings.

Serves 8

Chilled Salmon
(with Dill-Mayonnaise Chutney)
for a Summer Buffet or
for a Hot Summer Night Meal

1 cup dry white wine
1 tablespoon fresh dill
juice of 1 lemon
2-1/2 pounds salmon fillet (bones removed)
2 whole lemons, sliced thin

Combine wine, dill and lemon juice. Marinate salmon (cover and refrigerate) for 8 hours; turn occasionally.

Transfer salmon fillet to large sheet of heavy foil; discard marinade. Cover with half of lemon slices. Close foil tightly tent-like; place on cookie sheet.

Bake at 350 degrees for 20 minutes. Chill for 4 hours.

Line serving platter with fresh greens, garnish with remaining lemon. Add sprigs of fresh dill and parsley.

Serve with Dill-Mayonnaise Chutney (see recipe).

Serves 6 to 8

Dill-Mayonnaise Chutney

1/2 cup chutney (your choice — I prefer mango-based)
1/4 cup mayonnaise
2 tablespoons lemon juice
2 tablespoons fresh dill

   Mix all ingredients well; place in serving container and refrigerate. Can be sprinkled with capers. (Make a day ahead.)

   Makes about 1 cup

Grilled Salmon Fillets

Marinade:
1/2 cup white wine
2 tablespoons brown sugar
1 tablespoon minced fresh ginger
2 bay leaves
1/4 cup teriyaki sauce

3 tablespoons mayonnaise
2-1/2 pounds salmon fillets, (all bones removed) cut into 6
    serving portions

Garnish:
lemon slices, lime slices, kiwi slices, sprigs of fresh herbs

Combine all ingredients for marinade. Place salmon
fillets in container. Pour marinade over the fillets. Cover;
refrigerate for 4 to 8 hours. Turn twice.

Discard marinade. Pat fillets dry. Transfer to foil-
covered broiler pan.

With pastry brush, apply mayonnaise to each fillet.
With broiler on high, place in middle of oven. Broil for 10
to 12 minutes, or until lightly brown, and meat flakes
when prodded with fork. (Keep that piece for yourself!)

Garnish with lemon, lime, kiwi fruit, and fresh herbs
(if available). Can be served with Quick Hollandaise.

This is a last-minute dish, and a lot depends on how
well done you like your salmon cooked. I suggest not to
overcook, so that the salmon remains moist.

Serves 6

Indian Shrimp Curry
(with Seven Condiments)

4 tablespoons butter
1 large onion, finely chopped
6 stalks celery hearts, finely chopped
1/2 pound mushrooms, sliced
1 large Granny Smith apple, cored and diced
1/2 cup evaporated milk
1 tablespoon fresh curry powder (more if you prefer a
    spicier flavor) plus extra to serve at the table
2-1/2 pounds large cooked shrimp (about 6 to 8 shrimp per
    serving)

In a large dutch oven, melt butter; add onion and
celery. Sauté for 5 minutes; add mushrooms and sauté for
5 more minutes. Add diced apple.

Cover dutch oven and simmer for 3 minutes. Add
canned milk, and salt and pepper to taste. Add curry
powder; taste. (It is advisable to season mildly. Guests can
add more curry powder at the table to suit their taste.)
Store at this point or continue.

Before serving, let sauce come to a gentle boil; toss in
shrimp. Remove from heat. Do not cook any longer or
shrimp turn hard.

Serve over white steamed rice. Offer curry powder in
salt wells on the table.

Serve with Seven Condiments (next page).

Seven Condiments

8 ounces chutney (Colonel Grey's, or chutney of your
    choice, preferably mango-based)
2 hard-cooked eggs, chopped
6 ounces roasted peanuts, unsalted
6 ounces dark raisins
1 large firm banana, sliced fine
4 ounces coconut, shredded
1/2 cup green onions, green part only, chopped, or chives,
    snipped

Place each condiment in a small bowl on serving tray.
Pass tray for each guest to sprinkle chosen condiments
over shrimp/rice mixture.

Serves 8

Linguine with Rock Shrimp and Green Clam Sauce

4 cloves garlic, minced
1 large onion, minced
2 large green peppers, chopped
1 pound fresh mushrooms, sliced
2 tablespoons olive oil
3 to 4 tablespoons bacon bits, crumbled (optional)
2 tablespoons red wine vinegar
5 (6-1/2 -ounce) cans chopped clams
1-1/2 pounds rock shrimp
salt and pepper to taste
1-1/2 pounds fresh linguine
1 cup parmesan cheese
36 to 40 clams*

Sauté garlic, onions, peppers and mushrooms in olive oil for 8 minutes. Add bacon bits and vinegar. Add clams (with liquid) and rock shrimp. Let come to a quick boil; remove from heat immediately. Salt and pepper to taste.

Cook linguine according to directions; drain well but do not rinse.

Serve individual portions of linguine; top with clam sauce and sprinkle with parmesan cheese. Garnish with a few steamer clams around plate.

Serves 8

* To prepare steamer clams, see page 223.

Northwest Crab Cakes

1-1/2 pounds crabmeat, flaked and picked over
1 small red pepper, cored and chopped fine
2 shallots, chopped fine
1 tablespoon parsley (fresh), finely chopped
3/4 cup bread crumbs (unseasoned), plus some extra
1/2 cup mayonnaise
1 teaspoon Dijon mustard
1 tablespoon lemon juice
2 ounces butter
dash pepper; salt optional

Combine first eight ingredients. Gently form into patties. Coat with additional bread crumbs. Store or cook to serve.

You can prepare these two ways: frying or baking. Baking requires less butter.

To fry: In large skillet, at moderately high heat, melt 1 tablespoon butter till hot. Handle patties gently; they are fragile! Lightly brown for 2 to 3 minutes on each side. Turn gently! Remove to platter. Place in warming oven till ready to serve. Brown next batch. Serve.

To bake: Preheat oven to 375 degrees. Place crab cakes on buttered cookie sheet and bake for 15 to 20 minutes. Serve.

Serves 6 to 8

Soups

Farmers' Beef and Vegetable Soup

2 pounds lean stew beef, bite-sized cubes
2 (10-ounce) cans low-sodium, fat-free chicken broth
2 (10-ounce) cans beef broth
1-1/2 cups stewed tomatoes
1 large onion, sliced
1 cup celery, cut in chunks
1 cup mini carrots
1 cup green beans, in pieces
1 cup Brussels sprouts (optional)
1 clove garlic, cut in half
1 bay leaf
salt and pepper to taste

Place first six ingredients in 6-quart dutch oven (or soup pot) and let come to a boil. Simmer for 2 hours.

Add rest of ingredients and let simmer for another 20 minutes. The soup is now ready to serve or refrigerate for as long as two days, or it can be frozen. (Let soup come to room temperature before reheating.)

This is a soup with a "light" broth. If you want more stick-to-the-ribs substance, add 2 cups of cooked thin noodles, and it becomes Vegetable Beef Noodle Soup. Great either way!

Serves 6 to 8

Gazpacho Tureen

1 medium-sized green zucchini, chopped fine
1 medium-sized yellow zucchini, chopped fine
1 green bell pepper, chopped fine
1 red bell pepper, chopped fine
1 English cucumber (if you use a regular cucumber,
    remove seeds), chopped fine
1 large red onion, chopped fine
2 cloves garlic, minced
1 small jalapeño pepper, seeded and minced (wear gloves
    for this chore)
6 large ripe tomatoes, chopped
3 dashes Tabasco
1/2 teaspoon ground pepper
1 (32-ounce) can *V-8* juice
2 tablespoons fresh cilantro, finely chopped
salt (optional)
10 tablespoons sour cream
2 avocados, peeled and diced

   Combine all ingredients except for avocado and sour
cream; refrigerate for several hours. Can be prepared one
or two days ahead.
   Pour into individual soup bowls or cups. Serve with a
dollop of sour cream. Top with diced avocado. Great with
garlic bread.

   Serves 8 to 10

Texas Black Bean Soup

2 tablespoons butter
1 cup onion, finely chopped
1 cup green bell pepper, finely chopped
2 cans chicken broth (salt-free, fat-free)
2 (8-ounce) cans black beans
1/4 cup tomato paste
1/2 cup red wine
1 teaspoon cumin
2 teaspoons coarse black pepper
4 bay leaves
2 ounces butter
1-1/2 cup smoked ham, diced
Garnish:
1/2 cup chopped green onion
2 tablespoons chopped fresh cilantro (optional — some
    people just don't like cilantro!)

In heavy dutch oven, sauté onion and green bell pepper
in butter for 5 minutes; add remaining ingredients. Let
come to boil; reduce heat and simmer on low for 3 hours.
    Serve in individual soup cups or bowls. Garnish with
chopped onion and cilantro.

    Serves 6 to 8

Vegetables

Asparagus with Lemon Butter

1-1/2 pounds fresh asparagus (6 to 8 stalks per serving)
2 tablespoons butter
1 tablespoon lemon juice

Trim (or break off) tough ends of asparagus stalks.

Heat water in a large saucepan to a rolling boil. Place stalks in water and boil for 1 minute (no more!). Drain and cover with ice cubes until ice has melted. Pat dry and refrigerate till serving time.

Heat butter with lemon juice; pour over asparagus.

Serves 6 to 8

Brussels Sprouts and Carrots
with Orange Parsley Butter

Vegetables:
1 pound fresh Brussels sprouts
1/2 pound fresh baby carrots, cut in half lengthwise

Orange-Parsley Butter:
3 tablespoons butter or margarine
3 teaspoons grated orange peel
1 tablespoon fresh parsley, chopped
dash Tabasco sauce

Vegetables: (Microwave directions) Trim ends of Brussels sprouts; cut X in stem ends. Arrange Brussels sprouts and carrots in 2-quart microwave-safe casserole. Add 2 tablespoons water; cover. Microwave on high for 6 minutes, stirring once. Drain.

*Orange-Parsley Butter:*Place butter in small microwave-safe bowl. Microwave on high for 35 seconds or until butter is melted. Stir in orange peel, parsley, and Tabasco sauce. Pour over cooked vegetables.

Also delicious over prepared green beans and/or broccoli.

Serves 6 to 8

Grilled Stuffed Tomatoes

6 medium-sized tomatoes
2 tablespoons butter
2 shallots, minced
1/2 pound mushrooms
2 teaspoons Dijon mustard
1 tablespoon brandy
6 tablespoons parmesan cheese, grated

Cut off tops (about a quarter of the way down) of tomatoes; hollow out. (Save the pulp; put through sieve, allow moisture to drain, set aside.)

Sauté shallots and mushrooms in butter. Add mustard, brandy, and tomato pulp to mushroom mixture. Simmer for 5 minutes. Remove from heat. Let cool for 5 minutes. Fill tomato shells with mixture; top with parmesan, cover and refrigerate. (Prepare one day ahead.)

Before baking, let come to room temperature.

Bake at 375 degrees for 20 minutes.

Serves 6

Mashed Parsnip Potatoes

2 pounds red potatoes, peeled and quartered
3/4 cup parsnips, peeled and diced
3 tablespoons butter
1/4 cup heavy cream
salt and pepper to taste

Place potatoes and parsnips in 2-quart saucepan, cover with water, and let come to a boil. Cook for 20 to 30 minutes, until fork-tender. Drain well, place in food processor, blend till smooth. Add butter and cream; process until all ingredients are well blended. To reheat: Microwave for 2 to 3 minutes.

Serves 6 to 8

No-Fail Broccoli Soufflé

2 tablespoons butter
1 medium onion, finely chopped
2 (10-ounce) packages frozen broccoli, chopped, defrosted
     and drained
1 (8-ounce) jar *Cheez Whiz*
4 eggs, beaten
1 tablespoon *Wondra* flour

Sauté onion in butter until golden, about 6 minutes.
Add chopped broccoli. Remove skillet from heat; add
Cheez Whiz. Beat eggs with flour; fold into broccoli
mixture. Pour into buttered two-quart soufflé dish with 2-
1/2-inch rim.
     Bake at 350 degrees for 30 minutes, or until inserted
knife comes out clean.

Serves 6 to 8

No-Fail Spinach Soufflé

2 tablespoons butter
1 medium onion, chopped fine
2 (10-ounce) packages frozen spinach, defrosted and
    squeezed dry
1 (8-ounce) jar *Cheez Whiz*
salt and pepper to taste
4 eggs, beaten
1 tablespoon *Wondra* flour

Sauté onion in butter until golden. Add chopped spinach. Remove from heat; add *Cheez Whiz*. Beat eggs with flour, fold into spinach mixture. Pour into buttered two-quart soufflé dish.

Bake at 350 degrees for 30 minutes, or until inserted knife comes out clean.

Serves 6 to 8

Petite Parsley Potatoes

24 tiny red potatoes
1 tablespoon butter
2 tablespoons Italian parsley, freshly minced

With a potato peeler, remove one narrow strip of skin around the middle of each potato just for looks. Place potatoes in saucepan; cover with water. Bring to a boil and cook about 10 minutes, until semi-tender. Do not overcook.

Drain. Melt butter and drizzle over potatoes. Sprinkle with parsley; toss.

If prepared the day before, bring to room temperature and reheat in microwave on high for 2 minutes.

Serves 6 to 8

Spanakopita

2 (10-ounce) packages frozen spinach,
    defrosted and squeezed dry
8 ounces feta cheese
8 ounces cottage cheese (low fat)
4 eggs, beaten
1/2 teaspoon oregano
pepper to taste; salt optional
1 package phyllo dough, defrosted
4 ounces butter, melted

Combine first six ingredients in large bowl; mix well.

Remove phyllo dough from package, unroll and cover with a moist paper towel. (Cut phyllo sheets to fill size of baking pan.) Rewrap leftover phyllo, freeze and use another time.

With pastry brush, butter bottom of 9 x12-inch baking pan. Beginning with one sheet at a time, place sheet of phyllo in baking pan, and brush with butter; repeat eight times. (Handle phyllo gently — it is extremely fragile.)

Spread half of spinach filling on this first layer of phyllo. Repeat phyllo layer. Use rest of filling, and top with final layer of buttered phyllo, always using eight sheets per layer. Brush with remaining butter.

With a sharp knife, cut into nine equal servings (diagonally or rectangularly). Cover and refrigerate for next-day use. (Can be frozen, keeps well.)

Let come to room temperature. Bake at 375 degrees until golden brown, 25 to 30 minutes. Handle carefully; phyllo dough bakes "brittle."

Serves 8 to 10

Recipe Index

Appetizers

Breads and Spreads

Desserts

Meats

Meatless Meals

Poultry

Salads and Salad Dressings

Salsas, Sauces and Condiments

Seafood

Soups

Vegetables

To order additional copies of

The Nervous Hostess
Cookbook

Book: $16.95   Shipping/Handling $3.50

(503) 694-5381   Fax (503) 694-5046